FOR REFERENCE

NOT TO BE TAKEN FROM THE ROOM

Howard County Jewish Community School, Inc.
The Meeting House
5885 Robert Oliver Place
Columbia, Maryland 21045

FOR REFERENCE ONLY

The
INTERNATIONAL HEBREW HERITAGE LIBRARY

The INTERNATIONAL HEBREW

INTERNATIONAL BOOK CORPORATION
MIAMI, FLORIDA

HERITAGE

LIBRARY

By the Editors of
The Israeli Publishing Institute, Jerusalem, B. M.

VOLUME X:

GREAT JEWS IN SPORTS

EDITORIAL STAFF
for the International Hebrew Heritage Library

ORY N. MAZAR
General Editor

EMIL FEUERSTEIN, Ph. D.
Contributing Editor

GAALYAHU CORNFELD
MARVIN GROSSWIRTH
Editorial Directors

JOSEPH JARKON
Publication Director

CAROL S. SANDERS
Managing Editor

MILKA CIZIK
AMOS KAZIMIRSKI
Art and Production

Copyright © 1969 by International Book Corporation, Miami, Florida

All rights reserved, including the right to reproduce this book or portions thereof in any form.

Library of Congress Catalog Card Number 73-76566

Manufactured in the United States of America by Unibook, Inc., New York, New York

Table of Contents

	Page
Harold Abrahams	11
Abraham Attell	15
Arnold Auerbach	19
Victor Barna	23
Isaac Berger	27
Walter Blum	29
Harry Boykoff	33
Joe Choynski	35
Barney Dreyfuss	39
Bobby Fischer	43
Sidney Franklin	47
Benny Friedman	51
Marshall Goldberg	55
Hank Greenberg	57
Alfred Hajos	61
Nat Holman	65
Hirsch Jacobs	69
Irving Jaffee	73
Endre Kabos	77
Philip King	81
John Kling	85
Sandy Koufax	89
Emanuel Lasker	93
Suzanne Lenglen	97
Benny Leonard	101
Ted "Kid" Lewis	105
Sidney Luckman	109
Allen Maimon	113
Daniel Mendoza	117
Walter Miller	121
Lipman Pike	125
Myer Prinstein	129
Samuel Reshevsky	133
Mauri Rose	137
Barney Ross	139
Louis Rubinstein	143
The Runner of Afek	147
Dick Savitt	151
Adolph Schayes	155
Barney Sedran	159
Sylvia Wene	163
Henry Wittenberg	167

FOREWORD

The traditional Jewish love for scholarship is well known; so well known, in fact, that it has given rise to a myth: "Jews and sports don't mix."

That this is indeed a myth is borne out by the achievements of Jews in virtually every aspect of athletic competition. The first champion female bowler was a Jewish girl from Philadelphia. One of the world's greatest women tennis players came from a French-Jewish family. The annals of American baseball, football, basketball, track, horse racing and auto racing glow with names like Greenberg, Goldberg, Schayes, and Boykoff. Olympic medals have been awarded to Jewish athletes from the four corners of the world.

Even in athletic competition, Jews have been made aware of their religion. Anti-Semitism has often presented an obstacle to Jewish sportsmen. Seemingly, the same determination which makes a champion has enabled these heroes of the playing fields to surmount that obstacle and go on to claim the glory that is rightfully theirs.

Israel Renov, D.H.L., Ph.D.
Professor, City University of New York

ACKNOWLEDGEMENTS

The Editors wish to express their thanks to the various agencies and organizations whose invaluable assistance made this work possible. These include: The Zionist Archives, Jerusalem and New York; The Jewish National Fund, Jerusalem and New York; Keren Hayesod, Jerusalem; Beth Jabotinsky, Tel Aviv; YIVO Institute, New York; Union of American Hebrew Congregations, New York; New York Public Library; Hadassah, New York; The Nobel Foundation, Stockholm; The Leo Baeck Institute, New York; The National Foundation, New York; The New York Philharmonic Society; the Esperanto League for North America, New York; American Jewish Archives, Cincinnati; Jewish Theological Seminary, New York; and others. A detailed list of picture credits appears at the end of the Index.

Also gratefully acknowledged are the efforts and labors of Jeanne Kuebler, Eli Flatto, Barbara Northrop, and Joanna Smart for their editorial assistance; Amos Kasimirsky for work on production and layout; Charles Cassidy for special artwork; and Tove and Ira Solomon for additional research and photographs.

VOLUME X:
GREAT JEWS IN SPORTS

HAROLD ABRAHAMS
1899-

HAROLD ABRAHAMS

In 1920 Cambridge track star Harold Abrahams received a letter from the Amateur Athletic Association of Britain, informing him that he had been chosen to represent his country in the Olympic Games in Antwerp. Athletics was in the Abrahams family tradition, but although Harold was recognized as a star in college competition, he knew he had little chance of defeating the world's champion runners gathering in Belgium. He could run the 100-yard dash in 10 seconds and attain 22 feet 6 inches in the broad jump, but this was not enough. Harold learned much in the Olympic Games of 1920 and began a period of intense training in preparation for the games of 1924. In one sprint, he did the 100-yard dash in 9.6 seconds, a world record, but the wind was in his favor. Later, in a race in Stamford Bridge, Abrahams won with 9.9 seconds.

On going to Paris in 1924, Abrahams had no idea that he would return from the Olympiad with a coveted gold medal and an Olympic track record. Already he attained a speed of 10.6 seconds in the 100-meter dash, nine yards more than the 100-yard dash. But the American track team was favored to sweep the field.

As the day of the Olympics approached, Abrahams' coach gave final instructions to his pupil: at the start of the race he must not hold the upper part of his body too erect; must not wear new shoes; should moisten his neck and wrists with ice water; and above all, should start with lightning speed. Nervously, all the runners lined up. Paddock from America, Carr from Australia and athletes from Canada and the other Dominions. The starter appeared with his gun. Abrahams glanced at Carr, known for his brilliant starts. The starter fired his gun, and the runners leapt into motion. Abrahams realized with horror that his sidelong glance at Carr had cost him 1 1/2 yards and even as he started he was trailing the field. Panicked, he remembered the words of his trainer, "Never lose control over yourself, get your arms into motion... and forward!" Quickly and steadily Abrahams moved up, gaining inch after inch. Now he was almost even, then with new power surging through his body he was passing them, one by one, till suddenly to

Abrahams winning the 100-yard dash in an AAA Championship competition

his surprise he saw the goal before him and, chest extended, hurled himself against the ribbon of victory.

Abrahams won the 100-meter gold medal by two yards, and later received a silver medal as one of Britain's relay team in the 4 x 100 meter race. At home, in the same year, Abrahams established an English record of 24 feet 2 1/2 inches in the long jump, a mark that remained unequalled for 32 years.

His track career ended prematurely in 1925 when he broke a leg. Subsequently, Abrahams supplemented his profession of law with part-time sportswriting and broadcasting, and remained a distinguished figure in British athletic circles for many years.

ABRAHAM ATTELL
1884-

ABRAHAM ATTELL

Abe Attell, the famous featherweight, fought in 165 fights and came out of them without a mark — except for a broken nose, received when he was accidentally hit with a brick!

Light on his feet, with a sensational defense and a sparkling offense, "The Little Hebrew" won over $300,000 in his career at a time when boxers received little money. Every bout he fought in was calculated to advance his standing. Many times he carried his opponent to build him up for a return match, when Attell, an inveterate gambler, would bet huge amounts on himself.

Attell was born on Washington's birthday, February 22, 1884, and named Abraham Washington. Living in an Irish neighborhood in San Francisco, his training as a rough-and-tumble fighter came early. He claimed that as a youngster he fought three to ten times a day!

In the early part of his career, Attell was a slugger rather than a boxer. After his first 29 matches he decided that he was being hit too often and too hard and changed his style. He then concentrated on developing the ring craft and generalship for which he later became famous.

Attell became featherweight champion in 1901, a few months before his 18th birthday, defeating George Dixon in 15 rounds to win the title.

Attell was outspoken; he never hesitated to express his dissatisfaction if he thought decisions against him were wrong. In 1904 in a fight with Tommy Sullivan, Attell was knocked out in the fifth round but hotly contested the fight claiming that Sullivan was overweight. In the spring of that year, he met Sullivan again and knocked him out in the fourth round.

A month later, he fought a 15-round draw with Battling Nelson which Attell claimed he won. And on his 28th birthday, Attell lost the featherweight title to Johnny Kilbane. Again Attell maintained that he had been "robbed" and famous heavyweight Jim Jeffries backed him up. Attell's main contention was that Kilbane should have come after him because he was the challenger, but instead

ABRAHAM ATTELL

held back and took advantage of Attell's waning wind and legs.
 In his lifetime, Attell won 89, drew 17, lost 10. He won 46 fights by knockouts, and fought 49 no-decision contests. Damon

Abe Attell, left, battling Tommy Murphy

Runyon called him "one of the five greatest fighters of all time."

Abe Attell was a true artist of the ring, and is a member of the Boxing Hall of Fame.

ARNOLD AUERBACH
1918-

ARNOLD AUERBACH

When Arnold Red" Auerbach, fiery coach of the Boston Celtics from 1951 to 1966, retired to become Vice President and General Manager of the team, basketball fans from coast to coast lit up their cigars and blew a puff of smoke in tribute.

For Red Auerbach's victory-cigar act had infuriated fans for years (or delighted them, depending on whom they were rooting for). Only when he believed his team far enough ahead for a certain win, would Red relax and light up a cigar for the gallery.

In the hotly-fought world of professional basketball, studded with enduring and colorful personalities like Wilt Chamberlain and Bill Russell, Auerbach has been the most consistent performer of all.

In 1946, at the age of 28 and just out of the Navy, Red talked himself into the job of coach of the Washington Capitals. In 1951 he went to the Boston Celtics and started a long and uninterrupted career with the club. With the aid of Celtic stars Bob Cousy and Bill Russell, Auerbach established many precedents as coach.

One of his most notable exploits was in 1965. When Tommy Heinsohn was incapacitated by a foot injury, Auerbach replaced him with Willie Nauls, thereby fielding an all-Negro lineup. Up to that time it had been an unwritten law of the league never to star an all-Negro team because it might cut white attendance. Auerbach's lineup won 16 straight games with no drop in attendance figures. When he is asked why he did it, Auerbach explodes and delivers a speech that boils down to the fact that no one should confuse sound coaching principles with being a do-gooder.

Bill Russell once said: "When you get down to serious coaching, Auerbach is the best. He's versatile, intelligent, astute, flexible and he has me on the team. He is getting the maximum out of me. Red's an egotist, just like me. He is a human being. He keeps his failures to a minimum."

Auerbach in return observed, "I admire Russell because he's smart enough to understand me."

The team of Auerbach and Russell proved to be the key to an

ARNOLD AUERBACH

outstanding Celtic record. A championship had eluded Auerbach until Russell joined the club in 1956. From then on the Celtics became the team to beat. When he retired at 48, the only league

Coach Auerbach, with his constant cigar, poses with the victorious Celtics after winning their eighth straight Eastern Division championship in 1964

coaching marks left to be broken by Auerbach were those he already held. He had coached his team into eight world championships, 11 division titles and failed to make the play-off only once. He is the first coach in the game ever to win more than 1000 games.

Auerbach was born in Brooklyn, and attended George Washington University. He has toured for the U.S. State Department several times, and in 1964 introduced an NBA All-Star team to the U.S.S.R. He is the author of *Basketball for the Player, the Fan and the Coach*.

VICTOR BARNA
1911-

VICTOR BARNA

When Victor Barna was a teenager in his native Hungary, he saw his first ping-pong tournament. Two top stars of Hungary were playing. He decided then and there that there was nothing special in their techniques, and that he could work up to their level in a short time. Ping-pong was a sport which he enjoyed. He had first played when a friend, Laszlo Bellak, received a pair of rackets, a white ball and a net as a Bar Mitzvah gift. The two boys fastened the net to the dining room table and began to learn the game.

So began the saga of the world's best-known table-tennis player. Barna was champion at 19 and king of the sport for years to come, winning 22 world titles and more than 3000 prizes during a long and active career. Victor had also been a star soccer player on one of the Budapest teams. But the city schools prohibited pupils from participating in sports, so he had used a false name. When his team won an important game from a well-known rival, the losers threatened to reveal the truth to Barna's school. To retain his anonymity, the boy promised that he would not play soccer again.

In his first table tennis competition, Barna arrived early after a sleepless night, and found the auditorium still empty. In spite of his nervousness, he placed third. Two years later, he won the Hungarian youth championship. In the same year, the Hungarian school authorities gave him special permission to participate in the world table-tennis championship, which was to take place in Budapest. In this, although still a high school pupil, he won the doubles championship with another Hungarian star. By the end of the same year, Barna was ready to challenge Fred Perry, the English champion, for the singles title. He won, and became world's champion at the age of 19.

In 1934, Barna became the first European ping-pong player to tour the United States. For four weeks he and his doubles partner, Sandor Glancz, played before huge American crowds to thunderous rounds of applause.

Barna did much to popularize the sport of ping-pong throughout the world. In his prime, his technique and the brilliant precision of his movements were unforgettable.

Barna demonstrates his spectacular technique in this 1948 game in London

VICTOR BARNA

1935 was a fateful year for Barna. He had just won the world singles title for the fifth time. He had money and a luxurious car. Then, in a traffic accident, he sustained serious injuries, including a broken right hand. After operating, doctors told him he would never play ping-pong again. Barna did not believe them, and as soon as he was up and around, began to train with his racket. But he never again played with his former precision.

For several years following this misfortune, Barna's health and financial condition suffered. Friends said he looked 40 years old, although the accident occurred when he was 23. His marriage in 1940 changed things. Along with personal happiness, Barna got a ping-pong partner in the bargain. He and his wife became a successful table-tennis duo, traveling to many different countries, giving exhibitions. They won second place in the championship meet in India in 1949, and also placed second in the Irish championship in 1950.

When he was 38, Barna stopped participating in singles games, because the tempo of his game had decreased. But he continued competing in doubles tournaments until 1954. Today he serves as a trainer for English ping-pong teams, and is the author of several books, including *Table Tennis Today*.

ISAAC BERGER
1936-

ISAAC BERGER

Short of stature, light in weight, Isaac "Ike" Berger became obsessed with competitive sports as a teenager. Son of an ordained rabbi, he became a cantor and, in the synagogue, developed the breath control which would help him become one of the world's greatest weightlifters. He was the first featherweight in history to lift more than 800 pounds.

The immigrant from Palestine was, at the age of 20, the youngest weightlifter ever to carry the United States colors in an Olympic competition.

He started his career as a 4'11" youngster weighing 102 pounds. In four years of active work as a competing weightlifter he gained 30 pounds. In the Melbourne Olympics in 1956, Berger broke the world record to defeat the Russians with a lift af 776 1/2 pounds.

From 1956 he was undefeated in competition. It wasn't until 1960 that Minaev, the Russian champion, could beat him. Berger was a heavy favorite to win the gold medal in the Paris Olympics in 1960, but received a stunning setback when Minaev equalled his world record lift of 821 pounds to win. Even the Russian couldn't quite believe his victory, and called it a "gift from God." But Berger bounced back the following year when he went to Moscow and decisively beat Minaev.

Berger retired in 1962, tried a comeback in 1963, topping all existing world records. But in the 1964 Tokyo Olympics, he took a silver medal.

Berger's record is impressive: he is a member of the Weightlifting Hall of Fame. He won three Olympic medals in the featherweight division: gold in 1956 (776 1/2 pounds); silver in 1960 (798 3/4 pounds) and silver in 1964 (841 1/2 pounds).

He holds the world record in the featherweight division for the jerk, with 336 pounds, set in 1964.

WALTER BLUM
1934-

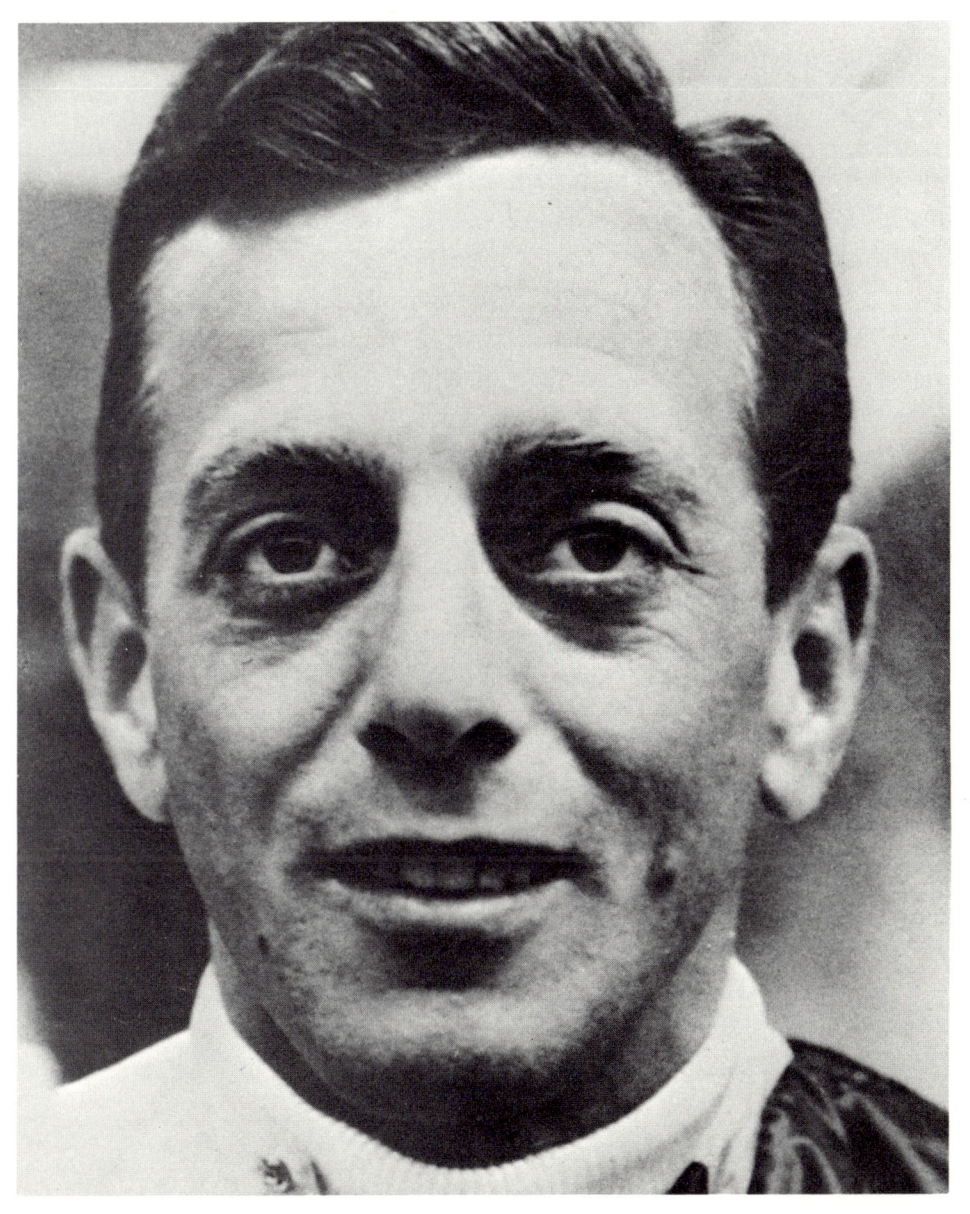

WALTER BLUM

From 1953 to 1964 Walter Blum won over $10,000,000 for his owners. But his name was comparatively unknown. He had very little of the kind of publicity top jockeys usually get.

Unspectacular, quiet, a family man, Blum never rode a top stakes horse, with the exception of Gun Bow. But he was National Riding Champion in 1963 and 1964. Also in 1964, he was winner of the George Woolf Award, presented to the jockey whose career has most reflected credit on his profession. Walter Blum was a high school dropout who rode for Hirsch Jacobs in 1951. When he rode his first winner on July 29, 1953, he promptly bought his contract from Jacobs in order to free-lance.

Since 1954, Blum has never had fewer than 1000 mounts a year. And in 1963, the year he was National Champion, his 1,704 mounts were the second highest number ever ridden by one man in one season. When the year closed he could boast of 360 winners. In 1964, he rode his 2000th winner home and finished the season with 324 wins. By 1968, he had his 3000th win. One of the top turf editors in the country said: "I rate Blum with the best three or four jockeys in the United States. He lets horses run — he doesn't try to strangle them."

In talking of his career, Walter Blum once said in an interview:

"I have no regrets. I'd do everything the same way if I had to begin all over again. I knew from the minute I came on the racetrack that this was the life I wanted. I guess it is unusual for a boy from New York to get into racing. Most of them never see a horse of any kind, much less a racing horse, the entire time they're growing up. As a rule, jockeys come from the Midwest and West where they learn to ride when they are very young. I had a friend who was exercising horses and he took me out to the track with him one day.

"Then Hirsch Jacobs gave me a job. I spent two years learning before I ever rode on a track. In those days trainers were stricter and you had to put in time before

WALTER BLUM

you ever got a chance to ride in a race. Nowadays, a rider can come on the track in the spring and be riding by fall.

Walter Blum on Troilus, March 3, 1959

"You grow up in a hurry around a racetrack. You'll find the jockey well traveled, at ease with people and able to converse well. They are much more mature and they'd better be gentlemen or they won't last long.

"Look around and you'll see that all jockeys are good athletes, wiry and healthy because they ride every day. But it's a very strenuous life, mentally and physically, and it gets you down after a while. You're bound to get hurt now and then, too. I broke my back in a spill in 1964."

Blum's accident spoiled his triumphant return to Santa Anita after an absence of 11 years. He left that track as an apprentice rider and returned as national champion, having achieved that honor for the second straight year.

HARRY BOYKOFF (1922-

HARRY BOYKOFF

Max Hodesblatt, formerly a basketball star for the City College of New York, was a teacher in the Department of Health Education at Thomas Jefferson High School in Brooklyn, New York. He was also the basketball coach and it was his job to build as outstanding a team as possible. So when young Harry Boykoff came to try out for the basketball team, the Coach sized up the boy's 6'9" frame and decided to mold him into a player.

To this day, Boykoff credits Coach Hodesblatt with making him a star. When he started on the Jefferson High team, he managed to score only one point in twenty games, but by graduation, Harry had been on the New York City All-Scholastic Team.

Boykoff enrolled in St. John's University in Brooklyn, winning national acclaim in his sophomore year when, on February 8, 1943, he scored forty-five points in a game against St. Joseph's College of Philadelphia.

America was at war and Boykoff entered the army in 1943 for a three-year hitch. He returned to college in 1946, but it was apparent that his military service had taken some of the steam out of him. His endurance and speed had been cut, but he was still one of the game's outstanding performers. He was captain of the team in the 1947 season and during that year scored 54 points in a Madison Square Garden game.

From 1948 to 1951, Boykoff played professionally. He then retired from the game, and is now a successful advertising executive in Memphis, Tennessee.

JOE CHOYNSKI
C. 1868-1943

JOE CHOYNSKI

A small group of men gathered on a barge off the coast of California on June 5, 1889. In the middle of the barge they left a clearing for the boxers. The air was charged with tension; the men were filled with anticipation, and also a bit of fear. They posted a lookout to warn themselves of approaching lawmen, for fighting of any sort was prohibited in those days, and even spectators might be thrown into jail.

The disagreement had developed a week earlier at the bank where Mr. Corbett and Mr. Choynski were employed. Mr. Corbett was boasting of his younger brother's prowess as a boxer and of the fighting ability of the Irish. Mr. Choynski also had a younger brother who could box well. Each man argued heatedly, trying to prove the superiority of his own brother. Finally, it was decided that the boxers themselves would settle the argument with their fists.

Thus Joe Choynski, a blond Jewish blacksmith, and Jim Corbett, a young Irishman, met on the barge. Both were amateurs at the time. The two young men looked each other over. Both of them liked to fight, simply for the sake of fighting. They eyed each other warily as each tried to size up the other to find the weak spots in his opponent's defense. The referee looked at his watch. The fight was on.

At first the contest was equal, for both were fresh and young. Joe Choynski's long blond hair blew in the wind. In later years his hair earned him the nickname of "Chrysanthemum Joe." Both boys were fast on their feet. At the end of the first two rounds, Joe Choynski's face was badly cut and blood was running into his eyes. Jim Corbett's hand, which was later to become famous, was hurt. By the end of the 14th round, Corbett's right thumb was broken. Then he received a staggering blow from Choynski, which all but finished him, but his brother pushed him on.

The fight went on this way for 27 rounds. In the 27th, Corbett was almost paralyzed, for both his hands were badly hurt. Choynski was breathing heavily, almost unconscious from pain and loss of blood. Then, Corbett tried one more left. His fist landed hard on Choynski's jaw and knocked him out.

As the spectators scurried forward to pick up Choynski and congratulate Corbett, they slipped on the bloody deck and fell. In later years, this fight would be remembered by both Corbett and Choynski as the hardest and longest fight they had ever been in or, indeed, had ever seen. Joe and Corbett fought five times in all.

Jim Jeffries (left) and Choynski square off for the camera

Corbett, of course, went on to become heavyweight champion, the famous "Gentleman Jim." Choynski never won an official championship, but was recognized as one of the greatest boxers of his time.

The list of other champions whom "Chrysanthemum Joe" encountered is a long one. He kayo'd Jack Johnson in three rounds in 1901; knocked down the great Bob Fitzsimmons, although the

JOE CHOYNSKI

fight ended in a draw; and forced Jim Jeffries, rated by many as the greatest of champions, to a draw in 1896.

Choynski was born in San Francisco, where his father was Collector of the Port during the Lincoln Administration and also operated a rare book store. Joe grew up in a scholarly atmosphere, meeting such literary figures as Bret Harte and Mark Twain, but his magnificent physique and a taste for rebellion led him to blacksmithing and the boxing ring. His career lasted 20 years, and his opponents were usually heavyweights with an advantage of 30 to 70 pounds. Choynski would have excelled as a light heavyweight, but this division was not created until 1903.

BARNEY DREYFUSS
1865-1932

BARNEY DREYFUSS

Why was Hazen "Kiki" Cuyler, star outfielder of the Pittsburgh Pirates, summarily benched during the entire 1927 World Series?

What could Cuyler have possibly done that was so bad that Barney Dreyfuss, Pittsburgh owner, would keep his powerhouse outfielder on the sidelines for the whole series? Particularly when the Yankees were clobbering the Pirates game after game? (The Yankees won the series in four straight.)

There was wide speculation, but one newspaper revealed that Dreyfuss had refused to play Cuyler because of a violent reaction Cuyler had to being fined $50 by the club. The star had let loose a stream of anti-Semitic invective at Dreyfuss' son, a Pirate executive.

It was believed that Dreyfuss benched Cuyler in retaliation, and kept him on the bench even though it probably cost Pittsburgh the Series.

This was typical of Barney Dreyfuss. Stubborn and high-principled, he was one of the most colorful club owners in organized baseball. He owned the Pittsburgh Pirates from 1900 to 1932, conceived the idea of the World Series, and built the first triple-decker park in steel.

Dreyfuss was born in Germany in 1865 which he left in 1882 to avoid military service. He came to the United States and took a job in a Kentucky distillery. Because of a health problem, it became apparent that Dreyfuss would have to be outdoors more, so he formed a semi-pro baseball team and played second base.

When the distillery relocated in Louisville, Dreyfuss moved with it and soon bought a share in the Louisville Colonels. However when Louisville was dropped from the National League, Dreyfuss bought a piece of the Pittsburgh Pirates. He rapidly moved the Pirates into a position of power in the National League with such stellar ballplayers as Honus Wagner and Rube Waddell, both of whom he brought along from Louisville.

In 1903, when the National League owners were involved in bitter battles with the new American League, Dreyfuss kicked over the traces and challenged Boston, the American League leaders, to a post-season series with Pittsburgh. This was the first modern World Series. Pittsburgh lost.

BARNEY DREYFUSS

In 1909, Dreyfuss opened Forbes Field, the first modern, triple-decker, all-steel baseball park. It was his tribute to the game's future and it remains as a tribute to him.

After the wounds of the inter-league fight healed a little, Dreyfuss became convinced that baseball needed a Commissioner with some strong powers and he fought for this innovation until his view prevailed.

A photograph of the first World Series game, at Boston's Huntington Avenue Baseball Park, 1903. As is shown here, a number of plays were interrupted by enthusiastic fans swarming on to the field

BARNEY DREYFUSS

In 1931 Dreyfuss suffered a tragic loss when his son died of pneumonia, and a year later, the grieving father passed away, too. Barney Dreyfuss was a baseball immortal — a history maker and an innovator.

BOBBY FISCHER
1943-

BOBBY FISCHER

Bobby Fischer was winning. It was humiliating to the 175 contestants in the 1958 U.S. Chess Championships, many of them with international status and titles, to lose to a mere child! The boy was the picture of concentration as he played. His game was complicated, and his reactions were often temperamental. Now, at 14, he had become the champion chess player of America.

A child chess prodigy is not remarkable, but national acclaim at such an early age is. Bobby learned to play chess when he was six years old. His 12-year-old sister bought a chess set, and decided to teach Bobby the game. It took him a little while to understand the rules and strategy, but then he quickly became an expert. When he was ten, he read a few books on chess, then re-read them and learned them almost by heart. His game improved as he experimented with the moves and problems.

Fischer won the U.S. Junior Championship in 1956, then the national title two years later. In his first try at international competition, he finished fifth. He took third place in Argentina in 1959, and later that year came in third at Zurich. Then, in 1960, he tied with the Russian champion Boris Spaski.

At the Chess Olympics at Leipzig, the American team, Fischer participating, took second place and the Russian first. By 1961 Bobby had won the American championship four years in a row, and repeated this feat each year he entered the tournament. In 1961 and 1962, he went undefeated in international competition — an achievement comparable to a new record in any other sport.

Perhaps because he has been famous and successful from an early age, and because chess is very important to him, Bobby Fischer has often been the center of controversy. He becomes angry, he sulks, and sometimes he refuses to compete. He has often had difficulty making himself understood by the world.

Once, after a world championship competition, he became angry and said he would not compete for the world title again. He claimed the Russians had decided on a champion among themselves before the tournament, and that all the Russian players had

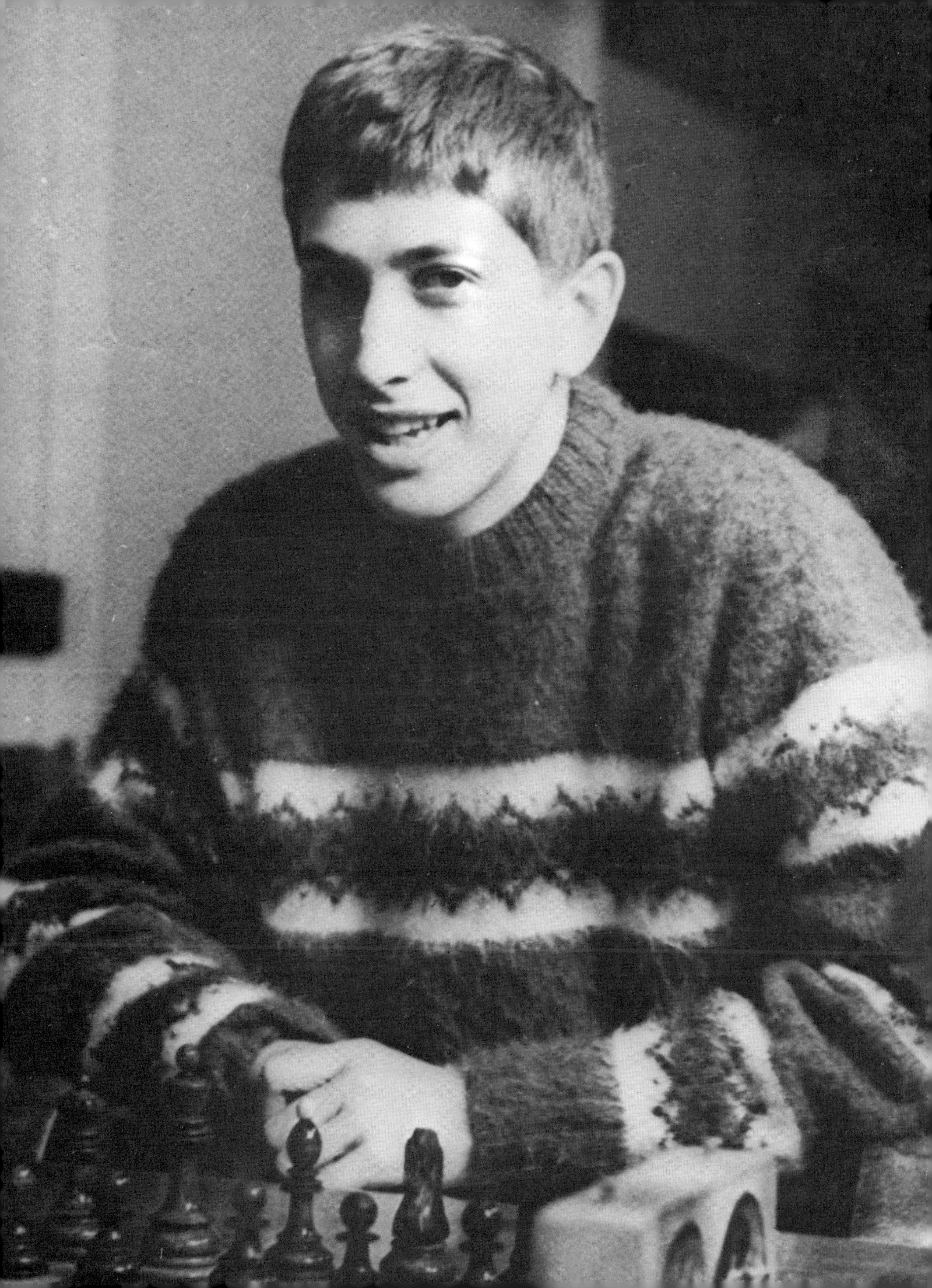

deliberately lost to this man, who was then fresh for his games with members of foreign teams. Fischer also claimed that the Russians had collaborated in calculating the moves, contrary to the rules.

Another time, an argument developed between Fischer and his fellow American, Reshevsky, at a 16-game competition in 1961. The 12th round fell on a Saturday. Reshevsky asked for, and was given, a postponement because of the Sabbath. Fischer then refused to attend on Sunday morning, saying he never played at such an early hour. The judges awarded the match to Reshevsky. Bobby, infuriated, protested the "loss," and refused to appear for any of the remaining games. Reshevsky was awarded them all by default.

When he was only 16, Bobby Fischer wrote a book, *Chess Games,* in which he describes his approach to chess and its problems. His technique is complex, and he feels that instinct and "feeling" are not enough. He has learned thousands of tried and tested chess openings and closings by heart. He is especially dangerous when a game is postponed. What might seem to be a loss or a draw, or a weak position, will in the continuation become something entirely different.

Fischer improves with age. Long before he was 30 he was considered America's strongest chess player. Experts predict he will be the first native-born American to bring home the world chess championship to the United States.

SIDNEY FRANKLIN
1905–

SIDNEY FRANKLIN

According to Sidney Franklin, the bullfighter from Brooklyn, his unusual career is the direct result of a teenage dispute with his father.

The senior Franklin came from Minsk, spoke eight languages, and had been appointed to the New York City Police Department by a commissioner named Teddy Roosevelt. He ruled his family of nine children with a stern and authoritarian hand. As Sidney put it, "When he said black was white, it had to be white." So, in 1922, Franklin left his studies at Columbia University and sailed for Mexico.

In Mexico City he was soon working as an illustrator, with a group of talented young Mexican artists. Many of their subjects depicted the bull ring. Franklin became more and more intrigued by the art of bullfighting. One day when a friend insisted that only a man with a Latin temperament could fight bulls, Franklin challenged him. He obtained an introduction to one of the great matadors of the time, Rodolfo Gaona, who liked the young American and offered to instruct him. In a few weeks Sidney was practicing with live bulls.

Franklin's debut as a bullfighter was slightly premature. An overzealous promoter had booked him for the bull ring on 48 hours notice, neglecting to consult Franklin about it. Franklin decided to fight anyway, and his career was launched. After several years spent acquiring a name for himself in Mexico, he headed for Spain in 1929.

When Franklin arrived in Spain he found his way to the United States Commissioner-General in Seville, the Spanish center of bullfighting. Thomas Campbell, the commissioner, put him in touch with Don Juan Abreau, who was in charge of the scheduling of bull ring amusements. How much money would the American ask to appear in the ring? When Franklin heard the proposition, he almost went back to Mexico. One thousand *pesetas* (about $150 in American money) was the purse. Who would pay for his quadrille of six men — *picadores, banderillos,* etc.? The best Seville would

Franklin, injured in an arena in Seville, is carried off to have his wounds dressed. He returned to kill the bull

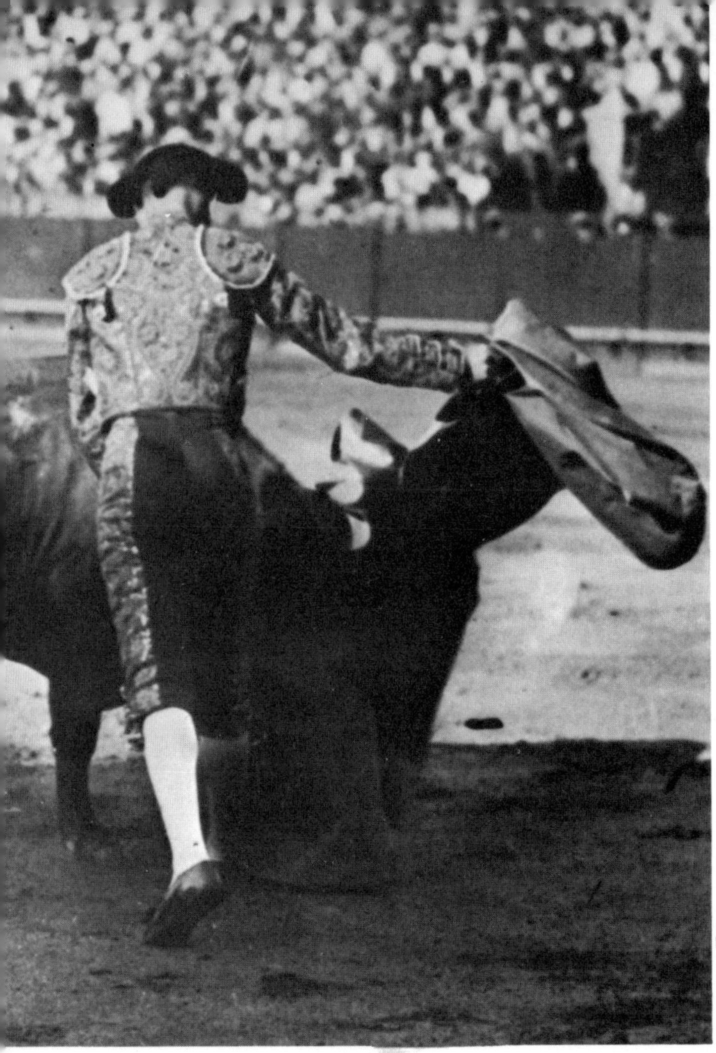
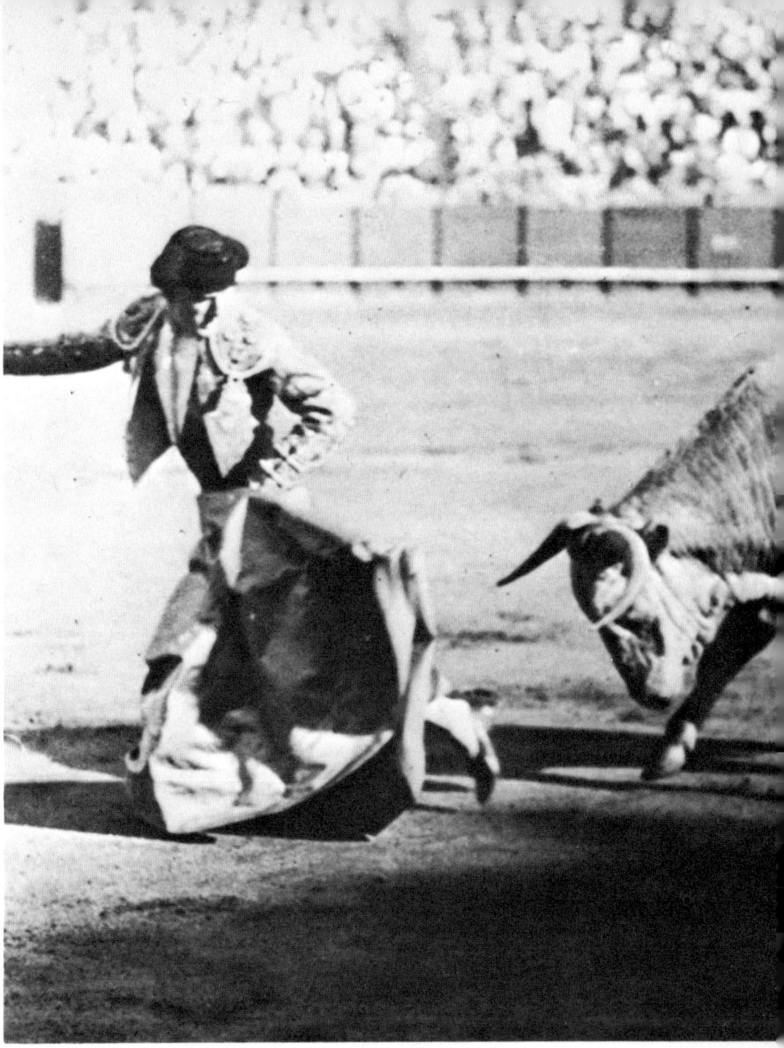
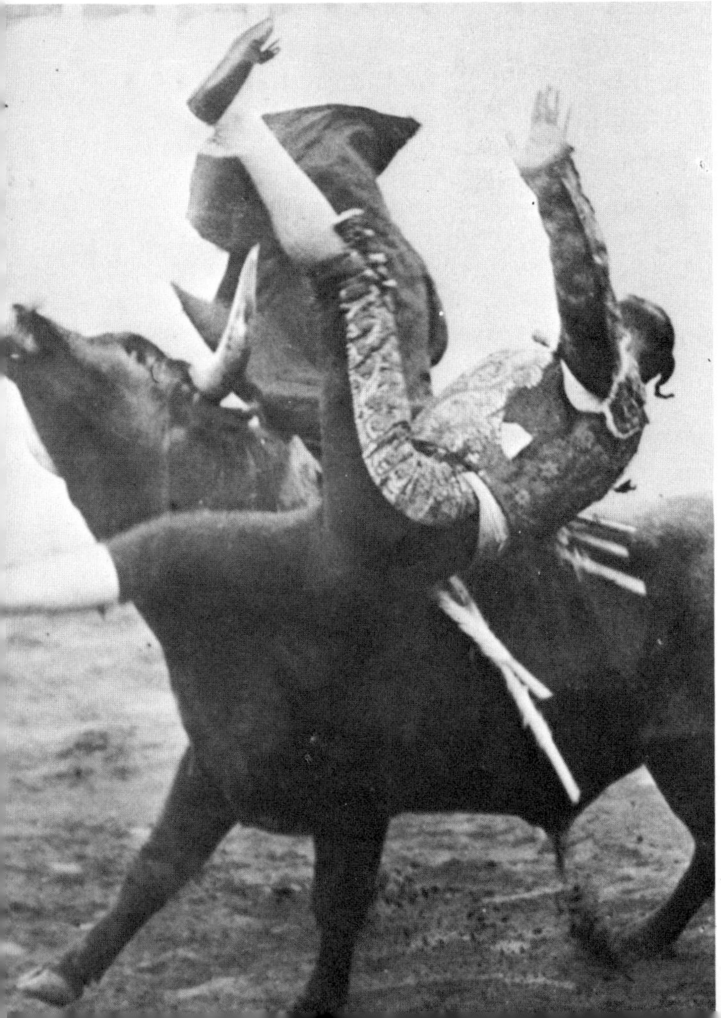
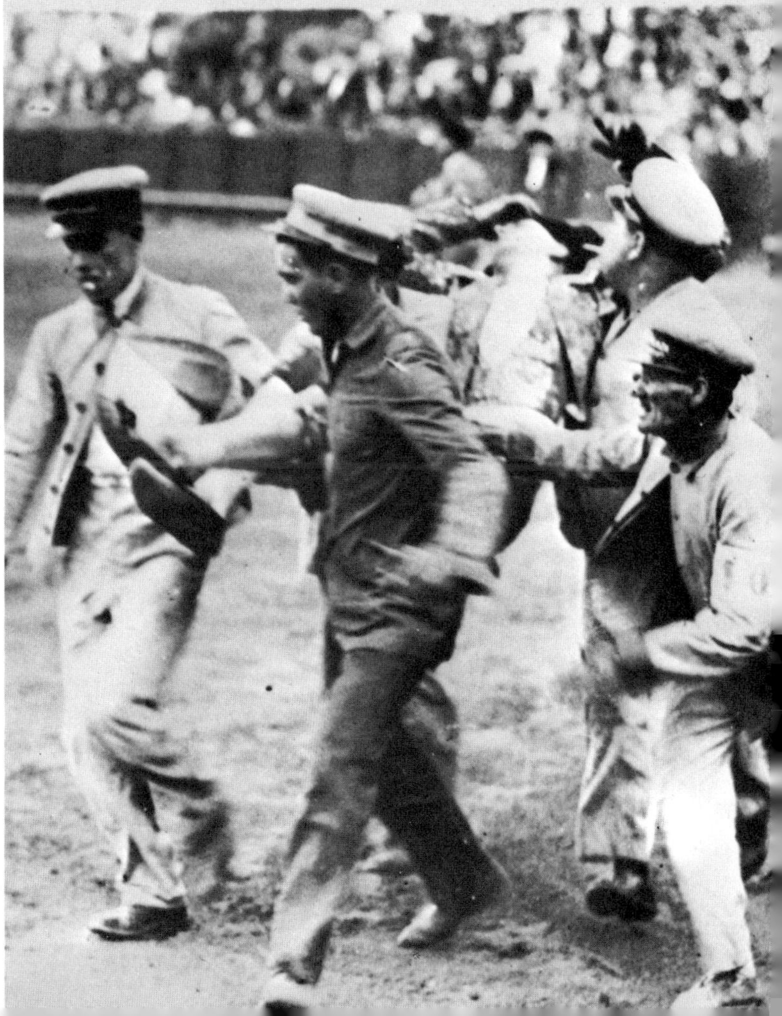

SIDNEY FRANKLIN

do was lend the American a quadrille made up of local boys, and promise $150 in cash, win or lose.

Franklin fought in Seville with his amateur entourage, and turned the town upside down by slaughtering two ferocious Andalusian bulls in one afternoon. The mob of fans swarmed down from the stands and carried him through the Prince's Gate, an honor accorded to only four matadors in history. And so Spain took the young lion from Brooklyn to its heart. He toured the Spanish bull ring circuit — Madrid, San Sebastian, Portugal and Spanish Morocco. Then he returned to Mexico, and went to Hollywood as a consultant in the making of films about bullfighting.

One of Franklin's greatest fans was Ernest Hemingway, whom he met in Madrid in 1929. As Franklin tells it:

> "Hemingway was in large part responsible for my success. He attached himself to a caravan of 20 to 25 cars of titled *aficionados* who followed me into the provinces. Since the fights were sold out, I couldn't get Hemingway tickets, so I smuggled him in as an assistant to the sword handler. He carried the sword case and water jug and then he'd stand behind one of the bluffers. I could fight the bulls, but I really didn't have the sense of drama to know what to do next to please the fans. So whenever I looked toward the crowd, I was really looking at Hemingway for signals."

Franklin was gored several times. His most serious injury occured in Spain in 1930. Contrary to doctor's orders, he returned to the ring five weeks later. His last accident was in Mexico in 1959.

Franklin has written an autobiography, *Bullfighter from Brooklyn,* and has operated a bullfight school in Madrid. He has also broadcast bullfights from Mexico. He became a full matador in Madrid in 1945, and remains the only non-Latin to prevail at "the moment of truth." Hemingway said of him, "Franklin is a better, more finished, more scientific matador than all but six of the best matadors in Spain today (1932) .... With the cape, he is a great and fine artist and no history of bullfighting can be complete unless it gives him the space he is entitled to."

BENNY FRIEDMAN
1905-

BENNY FRIEDMAN

He was the quarterback who "never made a mistake." Knute Rockne said he could hit a dime at 40 yards. Grantland Rice, in awarding him the All-American Quarterback spot in 1926, wrote: "For all-round football smartness and ability, you can't find a better man than Benny Friedman of Michigan."

Benny Friedman's football genius flashed across the nation's college gridirons from 1924 to 1926, and dazzled the professional game from 1927 to 1933. But he had a poor first season at the University of Michigan. He was benched for half the season by coach George Little and he played halfback the other half.

The following year Fielding Yost returned to coach the Wolverines (as the Michigan team is called) and molded a budding star into the total football player — superb passer, runner, blocker and kicker. With Friedman at the helm, Michigan sailed through the 1925 season undefeated until the annual big game against Northwestern University. The game was played in a howling 50 mile-an-hour gale in rain, hail, sleet and snow. Michigan lost 3-2.

This was the season that rocketed Friedman's name into the sports headlines. He did everything, and did it well: he passed brilliantly, developed cunning, on-the-spot strategy, and was on the tossing end of the famous Benny Friedman-Benny Oosterban forward pass combination.

In 1925, too, Friedman and Oosterban paid off an old debt when they toppled the Wisconsin team, which was then being coached by George Little, who had kept Benny on the bench that first year in Michigan. It was also the year that Friedman and company stopped the famous Red Grange and the Illinois team 3-0, with Friedman booting a field goal.

The rise of Benny's star in 1925 was pretty well dramatized by Grantland Rice's dilemma when it came to naming the recipient of his All-America quarterback award. Who should it be? Superlative ball carrier Red Grange or Friedman with his brilliant brain, superb passing and fine kicking? He gave the nod to Red Grange, but the next year he tapped Friedman for the spot.

BENNY FRIEDMAN

In 1926 Michigan drove through a tough schedule to the Big 10 Championship losing only to Navy 10-0. The high spot of the year was the Ohio State game which Michigan won 17-16 when Friedman gambled on a fourth down pass deep in Ohio territory.

In 1927, he turned professional with the Cleveland Indians and immediately electrified the fans by completing 11 out of 17 passes in his first game to beat the Giants 17-0. Actually, Friedman's lightning pass attack foretold the dazzling excitement of the football "air warfare" to come in the future. At that time, pro football was a crushing, bone-breaking confrontation between 200-pound players.

Friedman has the ball, but the Green Bay Packers are about to bring him down in this 1930 game

BENNY FRIEDMAN

After a mediocre season with the Indians, Friedman joined a new club called the Detroit Wolverines; it finished in second place. Friedman's next stop was the Polo Grounds in New York with the Giants, who wanted him so badly that they bought the whole Wolverine team, including the coach, to get him.

The Giants, just recovering from a disastrous four-win season, took off with the Friedman transfusion. They won 12 games in 1928.

In 1930, Friedman mixed his Giant chores with some backfield coaching at Yale University and in 1931, Knute Rockne, who had marveled at Benny's all-round ability, got a taste of the Friedman magic when he brought a Notre Dame All-Star Team to New York to play for charity. The Giants won 22-0. From 1931, and for the next three years, Benny shuttled between the Giants, his Yale coaching and the Brooklyn Dodgers. In 1934, he hung up his spikes as a player.

In 1941, he answered the call of New York's Mayor Fiorello La Guardia to coach at City College and in 1949, after he served in the Armed Forces, Friedman became head coach and athletic director at Brandeis University in Boston. He currently operates a boys' camp and is the author of a book, *The Passing Game*.

MARSHALL GOLDBERG
1918-

MARSHALL GOLDBERG

When Pittsburgh stunned the undefeated Notre Dame football team in 1936, beating them by a score of 26-0, there was much wailing and gnashing of teeth by Irish supporters. The thorn in their side was Marshall Goldberg, only two years earlier a high school star rumored to be headed for Notre Dame.

What might have been is written in the dazzling Goldberg statistics of that day. He scored himself. He passed for a touchdown. He almost ran a second half kickoff all the way back. On 22 tries, he gained 117 yards.

And Pittsburgh ended the season winning seven, tying one and losing one. Then they went on to win the Rose Bowl, 21-0, from Washington State. In 1937, Pittsburgh won the National Championship. Nobody could beat them and only Fordham held them to a tie. Once again Pitt slaughtered Notre Dame 21-6.

This was the year the Associated Press picked Goldberg as a halfback on their All-America team calling him, "The climax runner and sparkplug of the powerful Pitt array. Goldberg is a hard-driving, deceptive runner equally effective through tackle or around the end."

Strangely enough, Goldberg's professional career had little of the brilliance and promise it might have had. From 1939 to 1946, he played with the Cardinals. But even with the ferocious Goldberg drive, the team went nowhere. It wasn't until 1947 that they put together a championship team. But it was too late for Marshall. Due to a knee injury he was primarily used defensively. He tried one more year in 1948 and limited himself to defense with the result that many considered him to be the top defensive back in the game.

Today as an executive in a Chicago industrial plant, Goldberg looks back fondly on his football days as the crucible where he learned that singleness of purpose, the ability to get along with others, and recognizing the importance of victory can all be the making of a man.

HENRY "HANK" GREENBERG
1911-

HENRY "HANK" GREENBERG

It was July 1, 1945, and the Detroit ball park was packed to capacity. Everyone had come to see a returning hero play his first game since the end of the war. The air was electric with expectancy. Just before he had left for military service in World War II, "Hammerin' Hank" Greenberg had hit his 249th home run. He had not played now for four years, and today was the day he would try for his 250th. This was one game in a million, and thousands of Detroit baseball fans were there to see it.

The Detroit Tigers were in fine form that day. The excitement of the enthusiastic crowd had found its way into the pit, and when Hank Greenberg walked in, the players gave him a roaring welcome. Hank stood in the doorway, filled with emotion. He had been waiting for this day for four years of weary hardship and fear, serving as a captain in the Air Force in the China-Burma-India theater.

As he shook hands with his old friends and the new boys, he thought of the years of hard work and practice which had fixed him in the firmament of baseball's all-time stars. Hank had always been a good batter, but he was slow and clumsy when not at the plate. He had spent many full hours practicing at first base to improve his running time, his catching and his alertness. In short, he had been determined to become a good first baseman, and he had succeeded.

He had had many good seasons in baseball, and a few bad ones. His last season had been interrupted by the draft board. He was released from active duty only a few days before Pearl Harbor, and then volunteered again for active service when war with Japan was declared. Now he was back to take up unfinished business.

He glanced over the familiar furnishings of the locker room, remembering the season in 1934 when the Tigers came so close to winning the pennant. An important game had been scheduled on Rosh Hashanah. The whole country took sides on the issue, some saying he should not play, others urging him to do so. After much soul-searching, he decided to play that day. The two home

HENRY "HANK" GREENBERG

runs he hit helped win the game for the Tigers. Then another game was scheduled for Yom Kippur. This time he felt no hesitation: playing on one High Holy Day had been enough to satisfy his conscience. He spent all that Yom Kippur in his synagogue, and the Tigers lost the game — and with it, their first chance to win the pennant since 1909.

Hank Greenberg stops a grounder (1936)

HENRY "HANK" GREENBERG

Edgar Guest had written a poem immediately after Hank spent Yom Kippur fasting:

...Said Murphy to Mulrooney, "We shall lose the game today!
We shall miss him in the infield, and shall miss him at the bat,
But he's true to his religion — and I honor him for that!"

Hank walked out to the plate, took the bat in hand, and swung it back and forth a couple of times as he stood waiting for the pitch. His smashing hit sent the ball out over the field and into the bleachers. The tremendous crowd rose to their feet. "Run... run... !" and a few seconds later, "It's a home run!"

At the age of 34, "Hammerin' Hank" had scored his 250th homer. He continued to play for many more years, and then he spent his time teaching. Eventually he was elected to the Hall of Fame, the first Jewish baseball player to be given this honor.

The son of Rumanian immigrants, Greenberg was born in New York City, attended New York University for one semester, then left school to play in the minor leagues in 1930. He was with the Detroit Tigers from 1933 to 1946, and completed his playing career with the Pittsburgh Pirates in 1947. He was twice honored as the American League's most valuable player.

ALFRED HAJOS
1878-1955

ALFRED HAJOS

Hungary's first Olympic gold medalist, swimmer Alfred Hajos, was one of a number of Jewish sports stars participating in the first Olympiad of modern times, held in 1896 in Athens. His recollections of the event and further honors awarded him in the practice of his profession in architecture place him among the fathers of the Olympic tradition.

The last Olympic Games had been held in Ancient Greece in the year 389 A.D. After this, the Christian emperor Theodosius forbade them, for the games had become corrupted and he considered them a demonstration of pagan vanity.

In 1896, 1500 years later, 85 sportsmen from 13 countries gathered in Athens. In 43 events, Jewish sportsmen won nine gold medals, three silver medals, and three bronze medals. Three first places and one second place were won by the German Jew Flatow, while his brother, Felix, won two other firsts. An Austrian, Paul Neuman, won the 500-meter swimming race and two medals for cycle racing. The Hungarian student, Alfred Hajos won two events — the 100-meter swimming race and the 1200 meter swimming race. Twenty-eight years later in 1924, Hajos again participated as an architectural contestant in the first Spiritual Olympics. He won a silver medal for his plan of an athletic stadium in Budapest.

In 1946, Hajos recalled the 1896 Games:

"I remember that as 28 swimmers gathered for the race, they waved a huge American flag in front of Williams, the American, to encourage him. In my mind's eye, I saw the Hungarian flag as well, but on the top of the flagpole of victory! I was very excited. To this day I can feel the cold of the sea water on my skin. The competition was held in April, and the sea was ice-water. I swam with every ounce of my strength and only stopped when I heard the Hungarian team start cheering. That told me that I had won. The Greek Crown Prince himself raised the victory flag we had brought with us.

"The same day, the 1200-meter race was held. There wasn't much time to rest, and I went back to my place. Eight small

Alfred Hajos, at the age of 72, a successful architect in Budapest (1950)

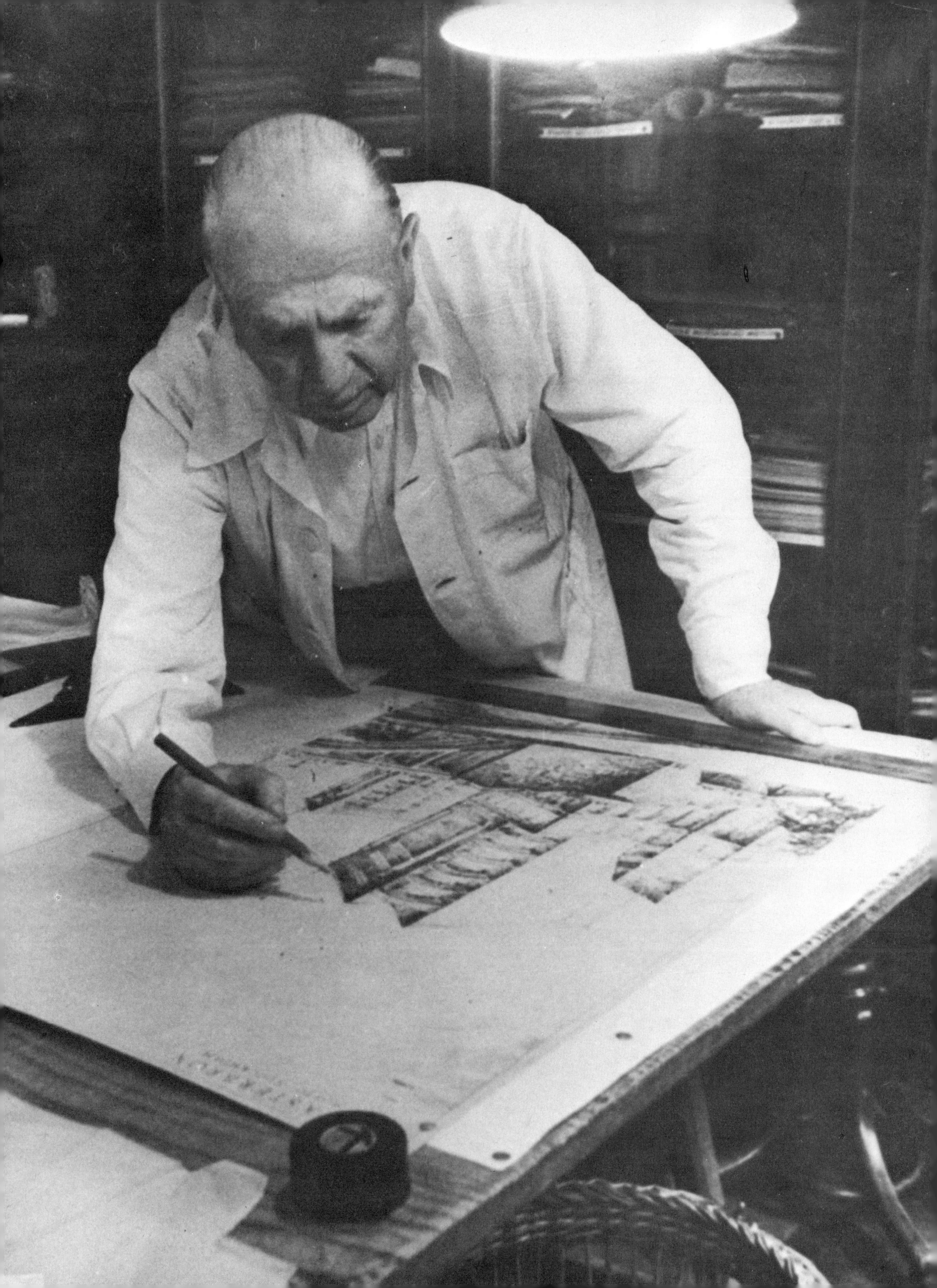

ALFRED HAJOS

motorboats took us out to the open sea. There were 31 swimmers taking part in the race. Although I had spread a layer of thick grease all over my body, I was frightened when the boats went back to shore. One after another, I saw my friends overcome by cramps because of the terrible cold. I felt all alone, abandoned in the open sea. It may be that this feeling brought me victory. I simply wanted to get back to shore as soon as possible. I swam strenuously, leaving everyone else behind. Again, the Hungarian flag was raised on the flagpole, this time even before I reached the beach. In 1924, the first Spiritual Olympics were held in Paris. I submitted my plan for a National Stadium, in Budapest, for which I won a silver medal. I think that I must be the only sportsman in the history of the Olympic Games who gained a medal in both the physical and the spiritual competitions."

Alfred Hajos was born Alfred Guttman. He changed his name for sports purposes, to sound more Hungarian. Hajos later established himself as an architect and built many important buildings, including hotels, schools and hospitals. In 1930, he was given a commission to build a covered swimming stadium on the Isle of Margaret, the beautiful Danube sports park in the heart of the Hungarian capital. Later he supervised the construction of the great stadium near Budapest whose design earned him his second Olympic triumph.

NAT HOLMAN
1896-

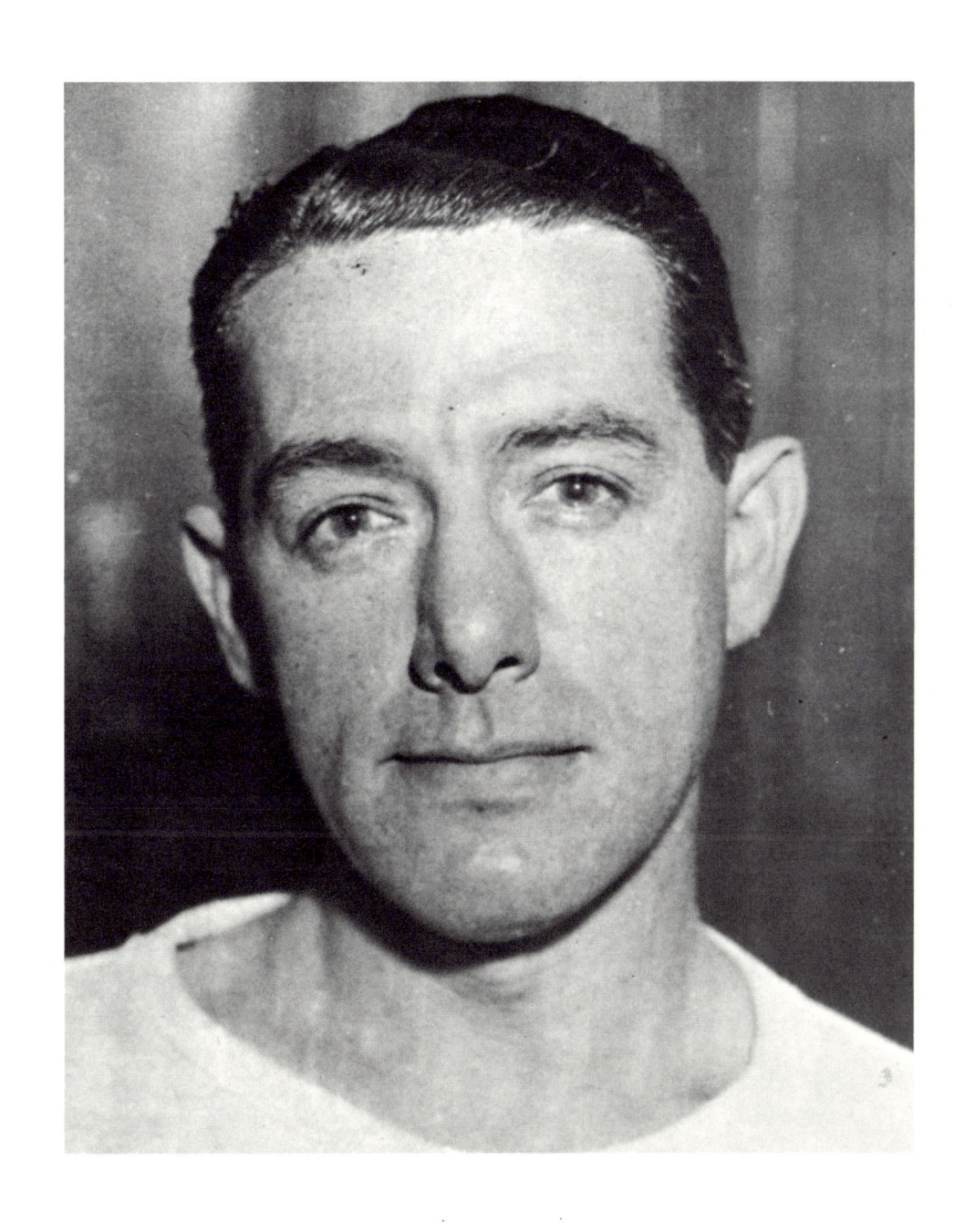

NAT HOLMAN

Nat Holman, "Mr. Basketball," was born on New York's Lower East Side, of Russian parents. He had six brothers who were all star athletes. Nat started his basketball career at the age of ten at a neighborhood playground. Coached by an instructor there who had been a professional basketball player, the boy went on to win letters in four different sports in high school, and matriculated at the Savage School for Physical Education.

He started his career in pro basketball with the Knickerbocker Big Five, who paid him $5 a game. While playing basketball and operating a children's camp, Holman was hired as instructor of hygiene and coach of the freshman soccer and basketball teams at the City College of New York. In 1919 he was named head basketball coach, the youngest college coach in the country at the time.

He continued to play basketball while coaching, and in 1920 and 1921 joined the New York Whirlwinds. With him on the team were the "Heavenly Twins" — Barney Sedran and Marty Friedman. Holman joined the original Celtics and stayed with the group until it broke up in 1929.

The Celtics were practically unbeatable. Holman's contribution to their success included a pivot play, which he invented, and which revolutionized the game. College coaches came to Celtics' games to watch and learn. Holman himself was an artist on the court. His dribbling and passing were flawless. He could shoot on the run with deadly accuracy. And he had the indefinable intuitive sense that anticipated an opponent's move split seconds before it happened.

Holman exhibited similar creative leadership as coach at CCNY. He built exceptional teams from 1923 to 1934. He still recalls the 1950 team that won the NCAA and National Invitational Tournaments as his best. But after the season, several members of the quintet were discovered to have been involved with gamblers. In the ensuing scandal, Holman was suspended and was not reinstated for two years, at which time he was completely vindicated.

Technically, Holman was caught napping only once in the 1939

NAT HOLMAN

season when a Stanford team hit New York and outmaneuvered and outshot his teams using a one-handed shot. This technique was counter to Holman's theories, which had become standard instruc-

The original Boston Celtics. Holman is in the center (1923)

tion all over the Eastern United States. It took several years for Eastern teams to master the New York style of play.

Holman has journeyed overseas for the United States State Department, and helped to organize basketball in Israel in 1949. He has conducted teaching programs in six countries, written four books, and made a movie called *Championship Basketball*. He was President of the National Collegiate Basketball Coaches Association, and was named the third greatest player of the half-century in a poll of sportswriters. Ed Wachter picked him for the All-Time All-Pro first team in 1941. He is also a member of the Naismith Memorial Hall of Fame and the Helms Hall of Fame.

HIRSCH JACOBS
1904–

He started out as a pigeon racer — and ended up training and breeding horses that brought in over $11,000,000. That's the incredible story of Hirsch Jacobs — the "voodoo veterinarian" — the man who can smell a winner in a "broken down nag."

Jacobs' first racing interest was as a teenager when he was fascinated with pigeon racing. His interest in birds lasted until he was in his early twenties when shortly after seeing his first horse race, he caught track fever. He quit his job and bought a horse called Reveillon.

In his first year, 1926, Jacobs made $200 with his one horse stable. The following year was not much better. But in 1928 he had 38 winners, earning a total of over $33,000. That proved to be a very important year for the young Jacobs. He was introduced to Isadore Bieber, who became his partner and who still shares the ownership of the Jacobs stable. Today, they own one of America's largest training and breeding operations. Their horses won more than 250 races and over $1,000,000 in 1962 alone. In 1964 the Jacobs stables topped all others with winnings of $1,001,643.

Jacobs has seldom been favored with horses who have great blood lines. He has been fantastically successful in turning seeming losers into winners.

The secret of his success seems to be a knack for bringing a horse to top form for a specific race. He reads more out of the condition book (a breakdown of scheduled races that comes out weeks in advance) than any man in the business. Some of the horses he has made famous are: Action, Paper Tiger, Palestinian and, of course, Stymie, his favorite.

Jacobs loves to tell the story of how he got Stymie for about the same amount he paid for his first horse, Reveillon. He spotted Stymie at Belmont in the spring of 1944. He was particularly struck by Stymie's appearance and the fact that he was a descendant of Equipoise, one of Jacobs' favorite horses. Then he noticed that Stymie, owned by the King Ranch, had a claiming price of $1,500. He rushed to the track and bought him. He learned later that some-

In the Winner's Circle at Suffolk Downs. Jockey Con McCreary is up on Stymie (1947)

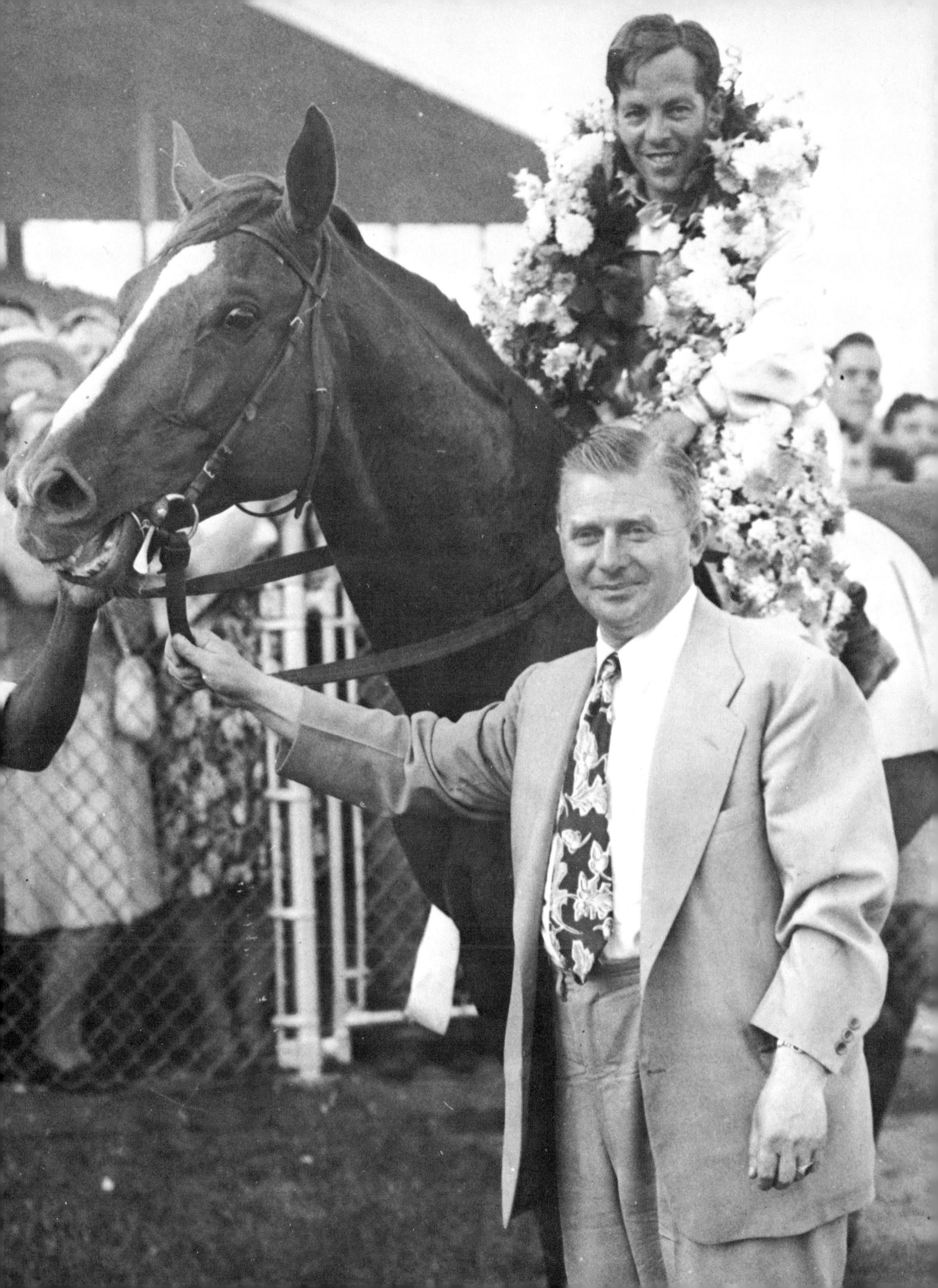

body had a small deposit on the horse and would have taken him away if he wasn't claimed.

Stymie raced 131 times and won $918,485, and when he was retired in 1949, he was racing's all-time money winner.

The Jacobs establishment is largely a family business. Jacobs races under the colors of his wife, Ethel. He has been assisted by his two sons. His two brothers are trainers. He was the top money-winning trainer in 1940 and 1960. His total of nearly 4000 winners is unequalled by any other trainer.

Hirsch Jacobs, the ex-steamfitter's assistant who raced pigeons from a New York rooftop as a boy, is today one of the outstanding figures of the Turf Hall of Fame.

IRVING B. JAFFEE
1906-

IRVING B. JAFFEE

Irv Jaffee was the ninth assistant bat boy for the New York Giants and ran errands for the regular bat boy. He was determined to become a professional ball player, but when he couldn't make the baseball team at his Bronx high school, he quit school. He switched to speed skating and went on to become America's greatest Winter Olympics champion.

When the Jaffee family came to the United States from Russia in 1896, the father was a pushcart peddler and Irving supplemented the family income with a newspaper delivery route. Walking, roller skating, and bicycle riding along his route helped to develop his leg muscles. It paid off handsomely when, at 14, he entered the Thursday-night indoor ice skating races at the Iceland Skating Rink in New York. But he was by no means an immediate success: he lost 22 straight races before Norval Bapte, a famous skater, took pity on the determined boy and took him in hand. Even with Bapte helping him, Jaffee had his troubles. He entered the Silver Skates in 1924 and missed. He lost again in 1925. Then, in 1926, he won the two mile Senior Championship, and the next year the world's record for the five mile at Lake Placid fell before his flashing skates.

At this point, it seemed that Jaffee was an easy choice for the Olympic team, but the Committee felt that he was comparatively untested in competition. And the Western interests weren't too pleased with the fact that Jaffee was an Easterner and a Jew. He was bitterly disappointed. Then suddenly there was an unexpected change of heart and Jaffee was told to get ready to leave with the team 24 hours before the boat sailed.

Jaffee placed fourth in the 5000 meter race, the best showing an American ever made in distance racing. He cracked the world record for the mile in a non-Olympic meet in Oslo.

In the 10,000 meter Olympic trials, Jaffee found himself racing against Bernt Evansen, Norway's world champion. After racing practically neck and neck for six miles, Jaffee's closing American-style kick took the match. Unfortunately, Jaffee was not destined

IRVING B. JAFFEE

to win the gold medal because after six races were run, the temperature rose — and the ice melted! Two races could not be run and the Norwegian referee ruled it no contest.

The whole city, including champion Evansen, picketed the official's hotel in protest against his denying the American the title, but the official refused to change his decision and Jaffee came home an unofficial winner.

Irving Jaffee leads the field during the 1932 Middle Atlantic Outdoor Speed Skating Races

IRVING B. JAFFEE

He went to work on Wall Street, where Emil Mosbacher, a stock broker, took an interest in him, and with several other broker friends financed his training at Lake Placid in preparation for the 1932 Olympic trials. However, Jaffee had to break training because of his mother's illness, and he was completely unprepared when the trials were held. He failed to qualify in the 500, 1500 or 5000 meter events, but finally won the 10,000. He had used the three shorter races for training. In the Olympics itself, Jaffee won the 5000 and the 10,000 meter events.

In 1934, he set a new record in the 25-mile skating marathon of one hour, 26 minutes, one-tenth second.

Today Irving Jaffee is winter sports director at a New York resort and helps to train U.S. Olympic teams.

ENDRE KABOS
1906-1944

ENDRE KABOS

The silence was deadly. Half the seats had emptied in the stadium. Endre Kabos of Hungary was to be awarded the Gold Medal for fencing at the 1936 Berlin Olympics, and many of the German spectators had left. The visitors sitting in the stands waited, uncertainly; then those who weren't Nazis began to applaud.

Many Jewish athletes had boycotted the Olympics. Two Austrian-Jewish swimmers, Judith Deutsch and Ruth Langer, were penalized for refusing to participate. But Endre Kabos was among those of his faith who came to Berlin to prove a point, and far from being brow-beaten by the hostile crowd, outdid himself in the competition.

Hungarians have always been outstanding fencers, and are especially noted for their ability with the saber. Fencing requires a quick eye and a well-coordinated and developed body. The expert must be able to attack and defend almost automatically. He is always studying his opponent and the sport requires intellect and careful strategy, as well as athletic ability.

In 1931, Kabos took second place in the European championship games. In 1932, he took first place in team saber and third place in individual saber at the Olympics. In 1933 and 1934, he was world saber champion. He went on to become World Olympic Champion, and this victory in 1936 also gave Hungary the team championship. The newspapers in Hungary could not praise Endre Kabos enough. After this high point, Kabos was European champion twice, and also won seven international competitions.

Endre had a charming style and personality. His performance in Stockholm, Sweden, earned him a Gold Cup — and a friendship that later saved his life. King Gustave of Sweden, in a burst of enthusiasm, made him a present of a gold ring and became quite friendly with the athlete.

World War II came, and Hungary joined forces with Germany. The Hungarians cooperated with the Nazis, and in 1943 adopted the Nuremberg Laws, which denied many rights to Jews. The Hungarian government made exceptions for international celebri-

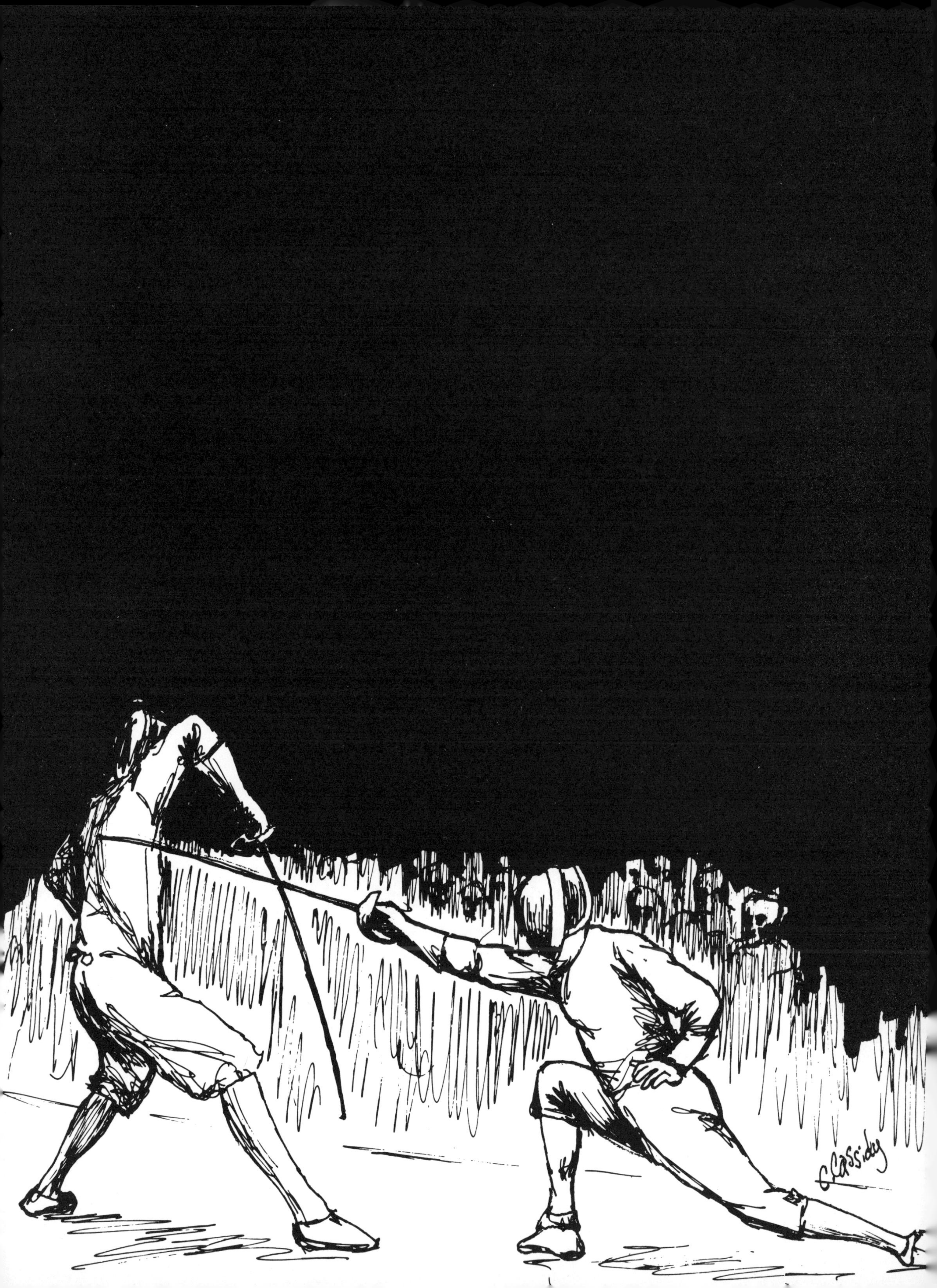

ENDRE KABOS

ties, such as Olympic champions. But by May 1944, being an Olympic champion was not enough. Endre Kabos was sent, together with several other athletes who had been left free until then, to a work camp. When the camp supervisor found out who Endre was, he "allowed" him to give fencing lessons to his soldiers. The threat in his voice was very clear.

"Sir," came Kabos' reply, "you can force me to do any kind of work, but you cannot force me to teach your men fencing."

Kabos was a leader of the work camp inmates and tried to keep everyone's spirits up. The story of the golden ring he wore was well-known. Not even the head guards would dare take away a king's gift. One day two letters came to the camp, one addressed to the commander, and one to Endre. The King of Sweden had written to the commander that he was arranging for Kabos' release. In the letter to Endre, King Gustave told Endre how much the Swedish people admired him, and asked him to be patient. Soon Kabos was allowed to leave the camp.

"I am ashamed," Kabos said to his fellow prisoners. "My place is with you." But he left. To volunteer to remain in a prison camp was pointless — it would accomplish nothing. After leaving the camp, he went into hiding, for the Hungarian Nazis had decided to rearrest him. In November 1944, the Hungarian reign of terror reached its peak. But Kabos escaped from the work camp in time — before it became a death camp.

Kabos was hiding in Budapest. He decided to go to Buda, on the far side of the Danube. He took an electric trolley across the Margit Bridge. Suddenly the trolley and bridge blew up. Accounts of this catastrophe conflict. One theory holds that the Germans blew up the bridge, and Kabos was killed accidently. Another theory is that Kabos blew up the bridge, and was killed trying to escape.

PHILIP KING
1872-1938

PHILIP KING

As a coach, he "framed" his team to put them on edge for their big game. As a player he scored as many as 11 touchdowns in one game. As Princeton captain and quarterback in 1891, he devised the forerunner of the modern double wingback formation.

Philip King made the Princeton freshman football team, as quarterback, weighing in at 138 pounds, in the then crunching game that was football before the days of the forward pass.

His first game was as a substitute for an injured halfback; he made two touchdowns and sparkled in sweeping runs around the end. It was in this season that he made 18 touchdowns in two successive weekends against Virginia and Columbia.

When the next season came, Princeton needed a quarterback. They decided to sacrifice King's scoring power for his field generalship, and assigned him the signal caller's spot.

He piloted the Princeton Tigers to an undefeated and unscored against record until they collided with the star-studded Yale juggernaut of 1891 with "Pudge" Heffelfinger, Frank Hinkey and "Bum" McClum. Yale won 19-6.

Even the veteran sportswriters were confused as to the proper place to put the talented young King. One well-known writer of the time said of the shift to quarterback, that Princeton lost a fine halfback but gained a great team captain and strategist. The very next season, he said that the best move King made was to put himself back in the halfback position.

In 1892, King was elected captain and drove Princeton to 11 straight victories without their goal line being crossed — until Penn beat them 6-4.

King returned to the quarterback position for the Yale game to protect an injured leg, but the New Haven group trounced the Tigers 12-0.

The next year, King piloted the Princeton team through an entire undefeated season and this time when they collided with a Yale team that had been undefeated in 37 games, the Tigers were ready. King unveiled an offense aimed directly at Yale's great end,

PHILIP KING

Hinkey. He utilized a formation where the ends dropped back. It was really the beginning of the double wingback formation that was to become so important in later years. Princeton won 6-0 and that touchdown was made circling the Hinkey end.

King became the Princeton coach in 1894, and from 1896 to 1902 he served as head coach of Wisconsin, operating successfully against the great Chicago, Minnesota and Michigan powerhouse teams.

Phil King in action against the Detroit Lions

It was when he was of Wisconsin that he "fixed" the officials in the game with the alumni so that the alumni won, and gave King the excuse he needed to scold a team he thought was becoming too confident. They won their big game against Northwestern 22-0.

After his stint with Wisconsin, King returned to Washington, D.C., where he ran his family's department store. But in 1903 he was back again coaching Georgetown and Princeton.

When football came under heavy attack and President Franklin D. Roosevelt called a conference of the top people in the sport, King was one of the consultants. Out of that conference came the beginnings of modern football.

JOHN G. KLING
1875-1947

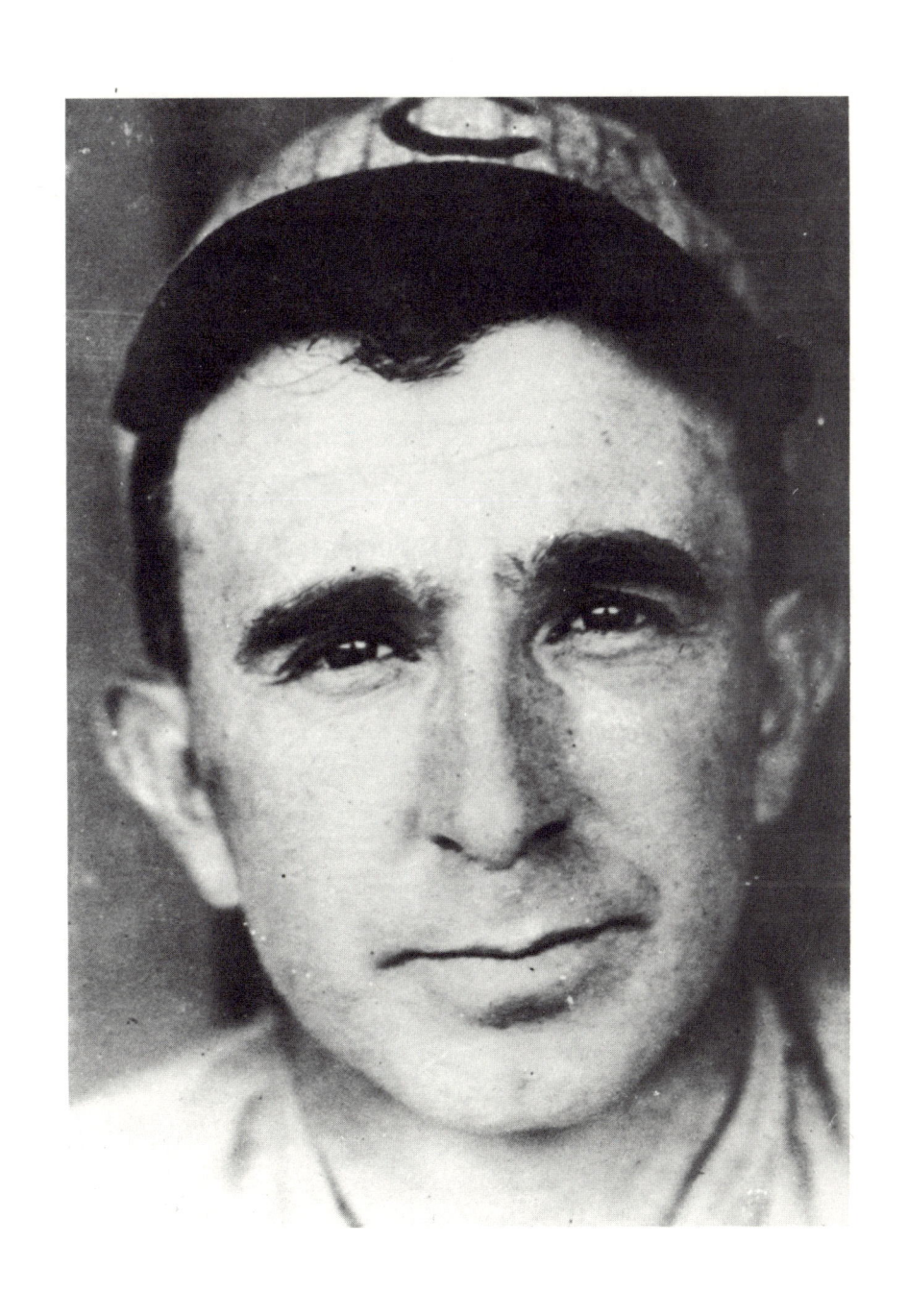

JOHN KLING

John Kling started out as a pitcher, but finished his career as one of the outstanding catchers of all time.

Born in Kansas City in 1875, Kling began his professional career in 1896 with Houston in the Texas League. He played some semi-pro ball, then in 1900 joined St. Joseph in the Western League.

Here, he was the rookie find of the year and quickly landed a spot in the majors with the Chicago Cubs, where he stayed for 11 years, through four pennants and two World Series.

Kling was used sparingly in his first year with the Cubs. The following year he shared the catching chores with the regular Cub catcher Frank Chance. After a couple of seasons, Chance moved to first base where he became one of the most talked-about stylists of the game, and anchor man for the famous "Tinker-to-Evers-to-Chance" double play combination.

Kling became a star in Chicago. He was one of the first catchers to throw from a crouching position and his lightning throws were easy to handle for he tossed a "light" ball. His powerful arm picked off careless base runners and would-be base-stealers with clock-like regularity.

In 1906 the Cubs won the National League pennant with an unprecedented 116 games, only to be upset in the World Series by the Chicago White Sox — who, at the time, were called "the Hitless Wonders."

The Cubs led the League again the next year. When they met Detroit in the 1907 World Series, Johnny Kling's arm and "throw-power" were pitted against Ty Cobb's daring and skill on the base paths.

In 1908, the National League season ended with the Cubs and the New York Giants in a dead heat. The tie-breaking game took place at the Polo Grounds on October 8, 1908, in an atmosphere of high tension. In this game, Kling's fast thinking paid off in the very first inning when, with men on first and second, and none out, he purposely dropped a third strike ball and lured Buck Hertzog into

Kling belts a home run

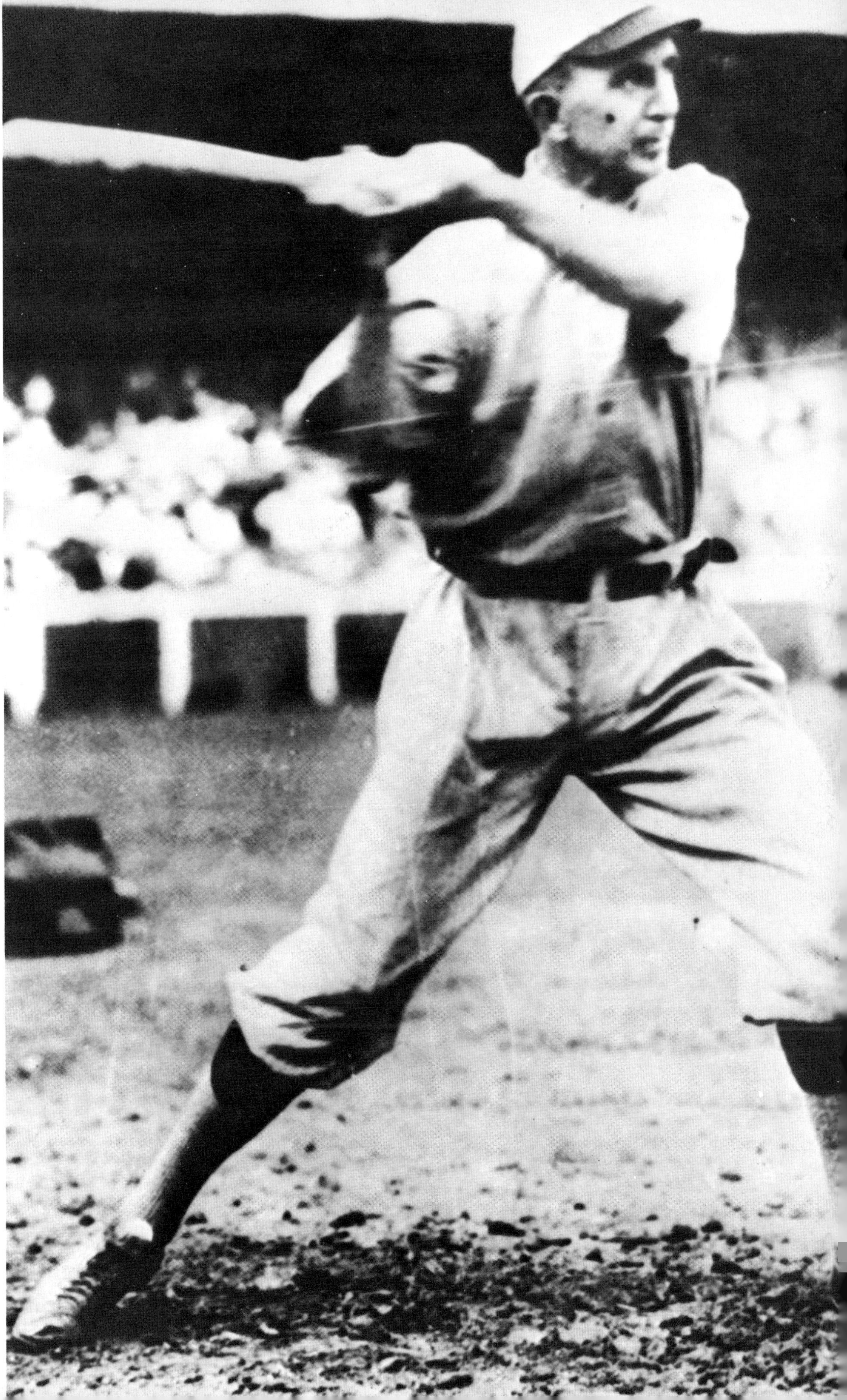

trying to steal, then easily threw him out.

The Cubs won 4 to 2 but the team left the field with a rampaging crowd of disappointed Giant rooters at their heels. They fled to the clubhouse where they remained until the police could bring the angry crowd under control.

The Cubs defeated Detroit again in 1909. That same year it looked as if Kling was going to retire because he decided to "hold out" for the year. He bought a billiard parlor in Kansas City and proceeded to win the World's Professional Billiard Championship himself.

In 1910 he rejoined the Cubs which had become a second place team in his year of absence. With Kling sparking them, they won the pennant again, but lost the Series to the Philadelphia Athletics.

Kling joined the Boston Braves in 1911. The Boston team spent the next two years in the cellar. When Joe Tinker, his friend and team mate from Chicago, was named manager of the Cincinnati Reds, he asked Kling to join the club. This was the last major league club berth for the Chicago star. He retired in 1915.

As one sportswriter put it, "Kling did everything well." He was highly successful with real estate investments. When he bought the Kansas City Blues in 1933, it only took him four years to build the franchise to a point where he could sell it to the Yankees at a handsome profit.

Kling died on January 31, 1947, an acknowledged master of his trade, leaving a legacy of grace and competence on the field for all who followed him.

SANDY KOUFAX
1935-

SANDY KOUFAX

Sanford (Sandy) Koufax was not only a very valuable member of the Los Angeles Dodgers — he was also the greatest Jewish pitcher in baseball. One of the most popular figures in the world of sports today, he was judged the National League's Most Valuable Player in 1963, and has achieved his fame in spite of a persistent crippling condition in his pitching arm that forced his premature retirement in 1965.

Like another baseball great, Hank Greenberg, Koufax caused his home team to look carefully at the calendar before scheduling important games during the Jewish High Holidays. Sandy asked to be excused from a game in 1961 because it fell on Yom Kippur. Dodger manager Walter Alston arranged for a substitute at the last minute, and Los Angeles lost the game.

When he was still a high school athlete in Brooklyn, Sandy Koufax's talents were noticed. They won him a basketball scholarship to the University of Cincinnati. He also went out for varsity baseball, and after his first year on the college diamond, received a shower of offers from professional scouts. Koufax had planned to be an architect, and had never dreamed of becoming a professional baseball player. However, in 1954, he signed a contract with the Dodgers which brought him back to familiar ground — the place where he had grown up and taken his first steps in sport — Brooklyn.

Sandy Koufax was only 19 years old when he signed with the Brooklyn Dodgers, and he wasn't quite ready for the challenge. He had talent — but very little experience or training. Years later, he recalled his first days as a professional: "I was so nervous and tense during the first week or so that I couldn't hold on to the ball. Once, when I wound up for a pitch, I made such a terrific effort that my arm was dislocated and I had to rest for a whole week."

Sandy kept on working to improve his game. There were ups and downs in his career, and he sometimes became discouraged and doubtful of his ability, but he stuck to his training schedules. His natural abilities, his devotion to the game, and steady training com-

Koufax leaps high in a vain attempt to catch a Philadelphia hit in a 1965 game

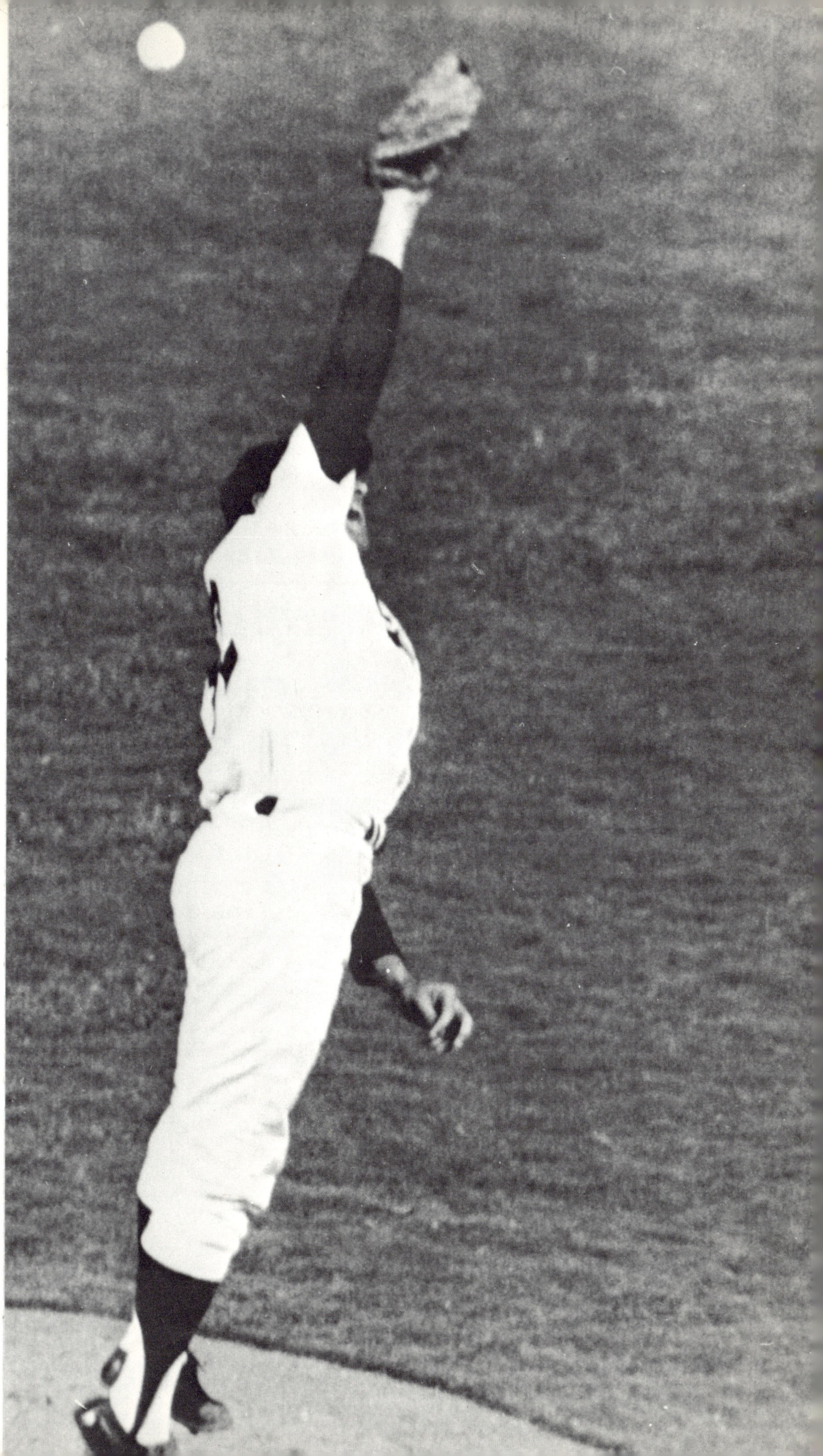

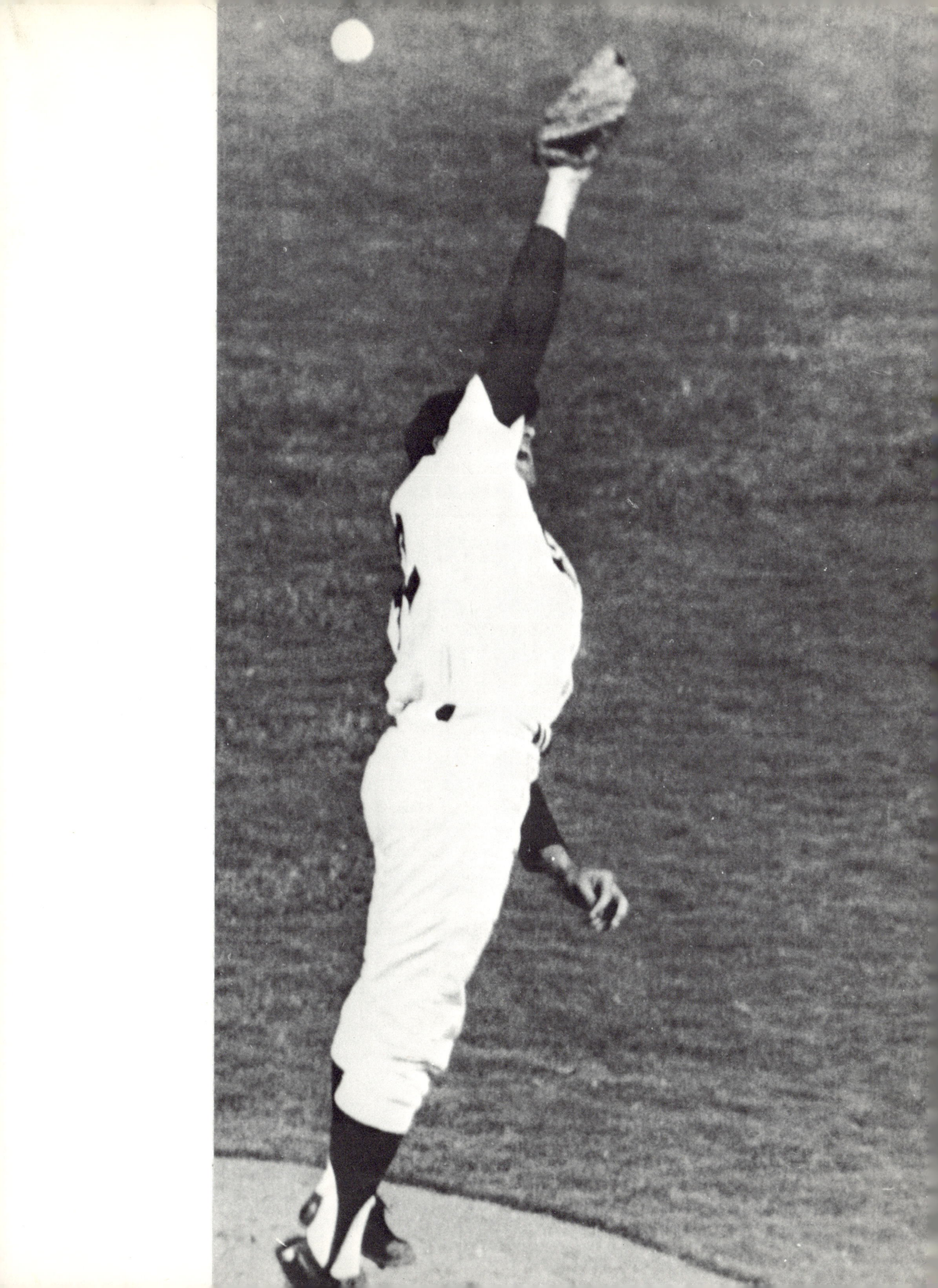

bined to make Koufax an outstanding pitcher. In 1961, he established a National League strike-out record of 269, beating the record of the legendary Christy Mathewson.

A year after this record season, a crisis threatened Koufax's career. One of his fingers became diseased, and he had to leave baseball for an entire season. Worse than being laid up was the knowledge that if his condition worsened, the doctors might have to amputate his finger to prevent the disease from spreading. Fate, however, was kind to him — he did not lose his finger, and he returned to the baseball diamond.

With renewed energy, Koufax won victory after victory for the Dodgers, who had moved to Los Angeles in 1958. Few pitchers have shown the control Sandy Koufax evidenced in the season of 1963. The accuracy of his pitching helped the Dodgers win 25 games, and the team went on to win the National League Pennant.

Honors and awards were lavished upon him, including the Cy Young Award as the outstanding major league pitcher of the year, and the Babe Ruth Award as the outstanding performer in the World Series. In addition, Koufax was the only athlete to be honored by the United Press, which praised him not only for his outstanding record, but also as "The athlete who has made the most impressive comeback in the Big Leagues."

Koufax during his prime was one of baseball's top attractions. He earned more than $ 70,000 a year, and sports experts estimated that his appearances drew up to 10,000 additional fans per game. He retired from the diamond after the World Series in 1965, but despite his abbreviated career, seems destined to occupy a place in baseball's Hall of Fame.

EMANUEL LASKER
1868-1941

EMANUEL LASKER

Everyone crowded around the two chess champions, trying to catch a glimpse of the game. The two men sat opposite each other, unmoving, the strain of concentration lining their faces. Two titans of chess were meeting across the board for the first time: William Steinitz and Emanuel Lasker.

Steinitz was the first player in the history of the game who could be called a "professional." He had held the world chess champion title for 28 successive years, and was known for his development of defensive tactics. Now, on that fateful day in 1894, he faced Emanuel Lasker, another formidable player half his age. Lasker won, and for 27 years — until 1921 — retained the title of world chess champion.

Emanuel Lasker was not a professional chess player, and although chess was one of his chief interests, he was involved in many other activities. He devoted much of his time to the study of mathematics and philosophy at several German universities.

He was born in Germany, and at the age of 14 started his career as a chess player, when he won a first prize in Berlin. Ten years later, he settled in England and won the British championship. A year later he became the chess champion of the United States. He was the owner of a unique record, as he was able to hold his championship title until 1904, when he tied with Janowski for second place. He was world champion from 1894 until 1921.

Lasker wrote two books on chess, *Common Sense in Chess* (1896), and *Lasker's Manual of Chess* (1934). In these works, he showed how mathematics could be used to calculate the most advantageous moves in a chess game. His interest in philosophy also showed in his chess books. He wrote, for example, that deception and falsehood, which seem to exist everywhere in everyday life, have no place in a chess game, where logic and truth are primary things. Another time, discussing the need to keep the chess pieces in constant action, he wrote: "Whatever is immobile must suffer violence. The light-winged bird will easily escape the huge hawk, although the hawk is larger. The firmly rooted large tree must remain where it is, and may have to give up its leaves, fruit and perhaps even its life."

Lasker's basic strategy was to study his opponent's style, watching for weakness. He would then take advantage of this weakness. Lasker personally felt that a player who does not play his "real" game until well into the match is pushed by his tardiness into working harder, and he will do better in the end. But a player who begins his game quickly, may rely too much on his early advantage and become careless. He felt that students of the game should obtain a feeling of self-confidence and rely on their own skills, rather than on devices like "openings." Contrary to other chess masters, he was opposed to learning game openings by heart. These become outmoded as new methods are developed. It is better, he believed, for the student to develop his own game and to obtain a sense of "balance."

For Emanuel Lasker, the important factors in determining the outcome of a chess game were the balance of forces, and the never-ending change in this balance. Each move creates new balances and counter-balances. Games cannot be determined in advance by certain set openings. A good player, according to Lasker, will study each new balance and look for some key or detail that will be beneficial to his game.

Lasker had many admirers, among whom were the readers of his books who not only learned the rudimentary techniques of chess, but also perhaps acquired some of the master's independence.

SUZANNE LENGLEN
1899-1938

SUZANNE LENGLEN

She burst out crying, "I can't, Father, I can't."

"Try again, dear. I say you must!"

The father was a stubborn man; the daughter was a very young girl. What he was asking seemed impossible. Monsieur Lenglen had decided that his daughter would become a champion tennis player and she did.

He had divided the tennis court next to their house in Compiegne into squares. Each square had a number painted on it. When Monsieur Lenglen called out a number, Suzanne attempted to hit the ball into the correct square. The child worked very hard, sometimes to the point of exhaustion, but she soon learned how to place a tennis shot with amazing accuracy.

When she was only 12 years old, she won first prize at the tennis matches at Cannes. Wherever she played tennis, her father was there, watching, encouraging, criticizing.

At 20, she went to Wimbledon to try for the international championship. Her opponent was Lambert Chambers, who had been a top seeded player for years. Everyone was sure the young French girl would be easily beaten, but she won the first set. Then Miss Chambers took the second set. Suzanne began to look very tired and seemed ready to admit defeat. Her father spoke to her encouragingly, and she returned to the court to win the championship, 9-7, 4-6, 10-8. The victory, and the dramatic circumstances surrounding it, made Suzanne a celebrity overnight.

A few years later Suzanne Lenglen competed at Forest Hills. Everything went wrong. She was sea-sick en route to the United States, and at Forest Hills, she discovered that the balls used in America were different from those in France. Moreover, her father had not been able to come.

She lost her first set, 2-6, to a player named Mallory. Suddenly her nerves gave way — she burst out crying and ran from the court. The gallery whistled and hooted. The newspapers called her behavior unsportsmanlike and predicted that she would quit at the first sign of pressure.

Mlle. Lenglen in an exhibition match on the roof of Selfridge's store in London (1934)

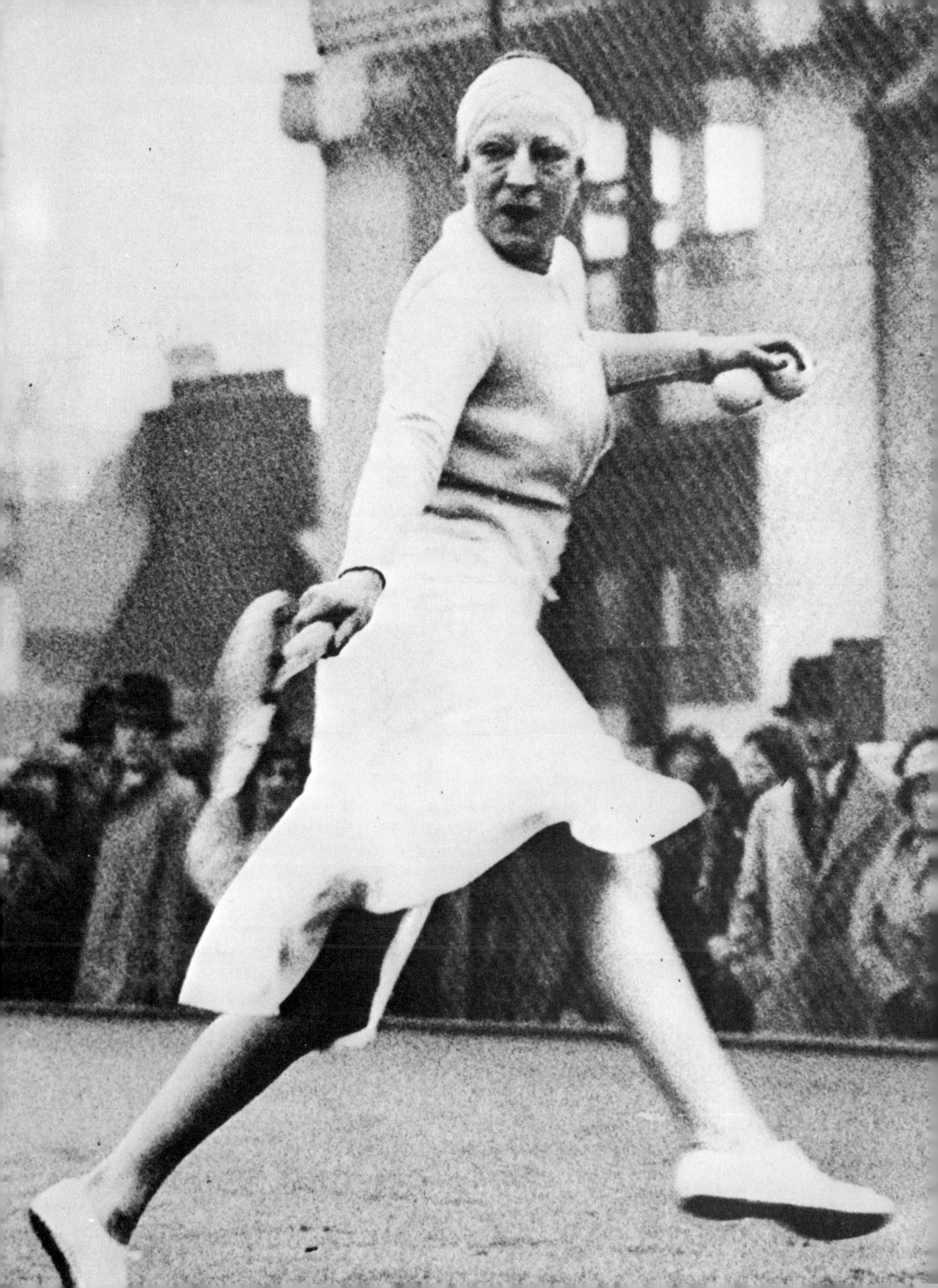

SUZANNE LENGLEN

However, in her next encounter with Miss Mallory, Suzanne dealt her opponent a smashing defeat in 26 minutes.

From 1920 on, she swept the matches at Wimbledon without a rival. In 1925, critics called her the best woman tennis player of all time. She was at the height of her skill. She won in singles, doubles, and mixed doubles. Her every match drew large crowds. Her most dramatic battle was with American tennis champion Helen Wills. The match drew enormous publicity. Headlines read "Two Queens at Cannes," for Miss Wills was considered the best American woman player. Fights broke out among the fans rushing to get into the stadium, people fainted in the crush. The King of Portugal, the Prince of Greece, and the Grand Duke of Russia were at courtside. Lenglen won, and when she arrived in Nice afterward, thousands crowded onto the streets and rooftops to cheer.

At her first professional appearance in Madison Square Garden in New York, 12,000 people came to see her play. This, and subsequent appearances, proved to be extremely successful financially. Suzanne's confidence increased, and she opened her own tennis school in Paris. In spite of a hot temper and nervousness, as a teacher she was known for endless patience.

Her name was magic to other tennis players as well as to the crowds. In 1932, the Frenchmen Borotra and Brogniogn were playing the Americans Allison and Van Ryn for the Wimbledon championship. In order to help French morale, Suzanne accepted the invitation to attend and flew to England, where she was given the use of the royal box. Her countrymen were so inspired by her presence that they played at the top of their form and won the championship.

She was not yet 40 years old when she died of cancer. Her greatest opponent, Helen Wills, said that Suzanne's intelligence, strategy and control of the ball had been unique. Her father got his wish: Suzanne Lenglen is still remembered as one of the finest players of her time.

BENNY LEONARD
1896-1947

BENNY LEONARD

New York's Lower East Side was a teeming mass of humanity at the turn of the century. Italians, Irish, Jews, swarmed into the United States and filled the seamy tenements of lower Manhattan.

Life was not easy. Most families were poor and hungry and from this hunger frustration and anger grew, anger which would lash out at almost anyone, especially anyone smaller and weaker, because it was important to feel superior in whatever way possible.

In those days, people who wanted to bathe went to public bath houses, and one group of boys took particular pleasure in terrorizing the Jews who lived on the street leading to the bath house. Then, one day, a boy named Benny Leiner, who lived on that same street, organized his friends into a small band of defenders. They headed off the gang of young toughs at the beginning of the street and showed them that they could not sail through, hurting and disturbing peaceful people for their own amusement. One of the many street brawls for which the Lower East Side was known broke out, but when it was over, Benny Leiner and his friends and neighbors were regarded with a new respect. This was the first "prize" Benny Leonard, as he was to be known professionally, ever won with his fists.

Benny changed his name because he did not want his parents to know that he was fighting for money. He could not keep the secret long, however, and when his family finally learned the truth, they reluctantly allowed him to pursue his chosen career.

The decision was a wise one, for Benny Leonard proved to be one of the finest and most popular boxers in the history of the ring.

Leonard's first professional fight, in 1911, was stopped in the middle because, although he was winning, his nose was bleeding badly. He earned four dollars for that fight. For the next five years, Benny fought a number of bouts, most of them minor, winning all but two. Then, in 1916, his big chance came: he met Freddy Welsh, of England, lightweight champion of the world. In those days, boxing matches were not settled by "decisions"; a challenger needed a knockout to win. Technically, therefore, Leonard lost. They met again later that year and Welsh soundly beat Leonard, but on May 28, 1917, Benny finally wrested the championship from Welsh, to keep it until his retirement in 1925.

Benny Leonard (left) squares off with Jack Dempsey for the benefit of young army recruits

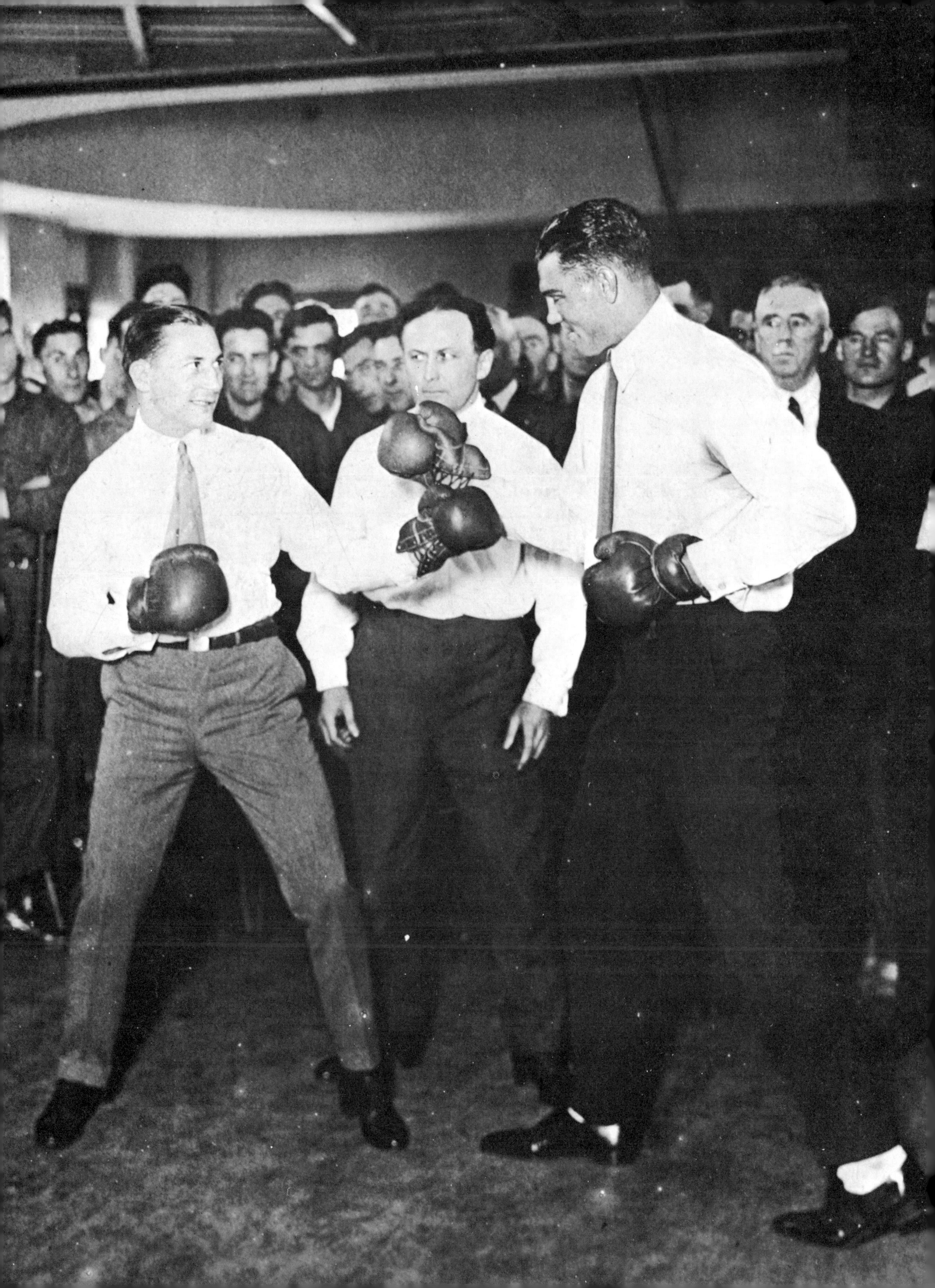

BENNY LEONARD

Leonard appeared in the ring fifteen more times in 1917, while at the same time helping America's war effort. The United States had entered World War I and Benny Leonard traveled to army camps giving soldiers boxing lessons, staging exhibition fights, and helping to sell war bonds.

Leonard's star continued to rise. He became famous as a "scientific" fighter who carefully studied his opponent's technique and habits and could, therefore, usually find a weak point to penetrate.

In 1922, he entered the welterweight class in a fight against champion Jack Britton. It was one of his worst fights and he was disqualified because of a foul. In the summer of 1922, he fought Lew Tendler in his own class for the title and although the fight went badly, Leonard retained the championship because he had not been knocked down. The following year, however, they met again, and Leonard gave Tendler a fifteen-round boxing lesson.

Benny fought two more bouts after that; then, in deference to the pleadings of his ailing mother, he retired from the ring in 1925, with a million dollars. His wealth was shortlived, however; the stock market crash of 1929 wiped out his entire fortune. Seven years after his retirement, Benny Leonard was forced, by financial setback, to return to the ring. It was a mistake. On October 7, 1932, Benny was knocked out in the sixth round by Jimmy McLarnin and retired for the second—and final—time.

He again served his nation's war effort in World War II as a Lieutenant Commander in the U.S. Merchant Marine, again as a boxing instructor. In 1943, he became a referee and four years later, on April 18, 1947, died in the ring while performing that function.

Benny Leonard fought 209 professional matches, losing only five. He was regarded as one of the finest boxers in the history of the sport, and never forgot his background or his origins. During his lifetime he supported many Jewish causes and remained devoted to his people and his family. Nat Fleischer wrote a biography about him, the title of which seems to sum up the man which Benny Leiner grew up to be—*Leonard the Magnificent*.

TED LEWIS
1893-

TED "KID" LEWIS

Ted "Kid" Lewis was one of the great boxers in the history of the sport. He fought in the ring for 20 years — from 1910 to 1930 — losing only 24 fights out of 250. Lewis was one of a number of Jewish lightweight and welterweight title holders, including Daniel Mendoza, the first Jewish world champion; Jackie Fields, Olympic featherweight champion; Barney Ross, the only Jew to hold both the lightweight and welterweight titles; and Benny Leonard, the first Jewish lightweight champion. Lewis also held the world lightweight title and was British champion in various weight divisions, writing an unforgettable chapter in the history of British boxing.

Ted Lewis, whom American ring fans nicknamed "Kid," was born Gershon Mendeloff, the son of a London cabinetmaker. He decided to call himself Lewis after a Jewish fighter named Harry Lewis whom he admired. Like most Jewish boys growing up in the slums, Ted knew how to defend himself. He showed unusual talent with his fists, and by the time he was 15 he was putting on exhibition fights before paid audiences. During those years, while he was developing his abilities and had no money, he would hold a fight for a shilling, a cup of coffee, or a piece of cake. In Whitechapel Road there was a tavern where boxing matches were often held. Here Ted made such a name for himself that soon he was earning 30 shillings a fight.

His career accelerated with dizzying speed, and when he was 17, Lewis captured the British featherweight title from Alec Lambert. Soon after, he won the Australian championship, and then the European championship. These titles marked the beginning of a phenomenal saga in the ring, in which Lewis started at 125 pounds, and finished as a 170-pounder, fighting heavyweights.

It was only natural that the classic land of boxing, the United States, wanted to see Lewis fight, and Lewis' success in America was beyond all expectations. When he defeated Willy Rudi in 1915 to become World Lightweight Champion, his immortality was assured. The United States was also the scene of Lewis' marathon

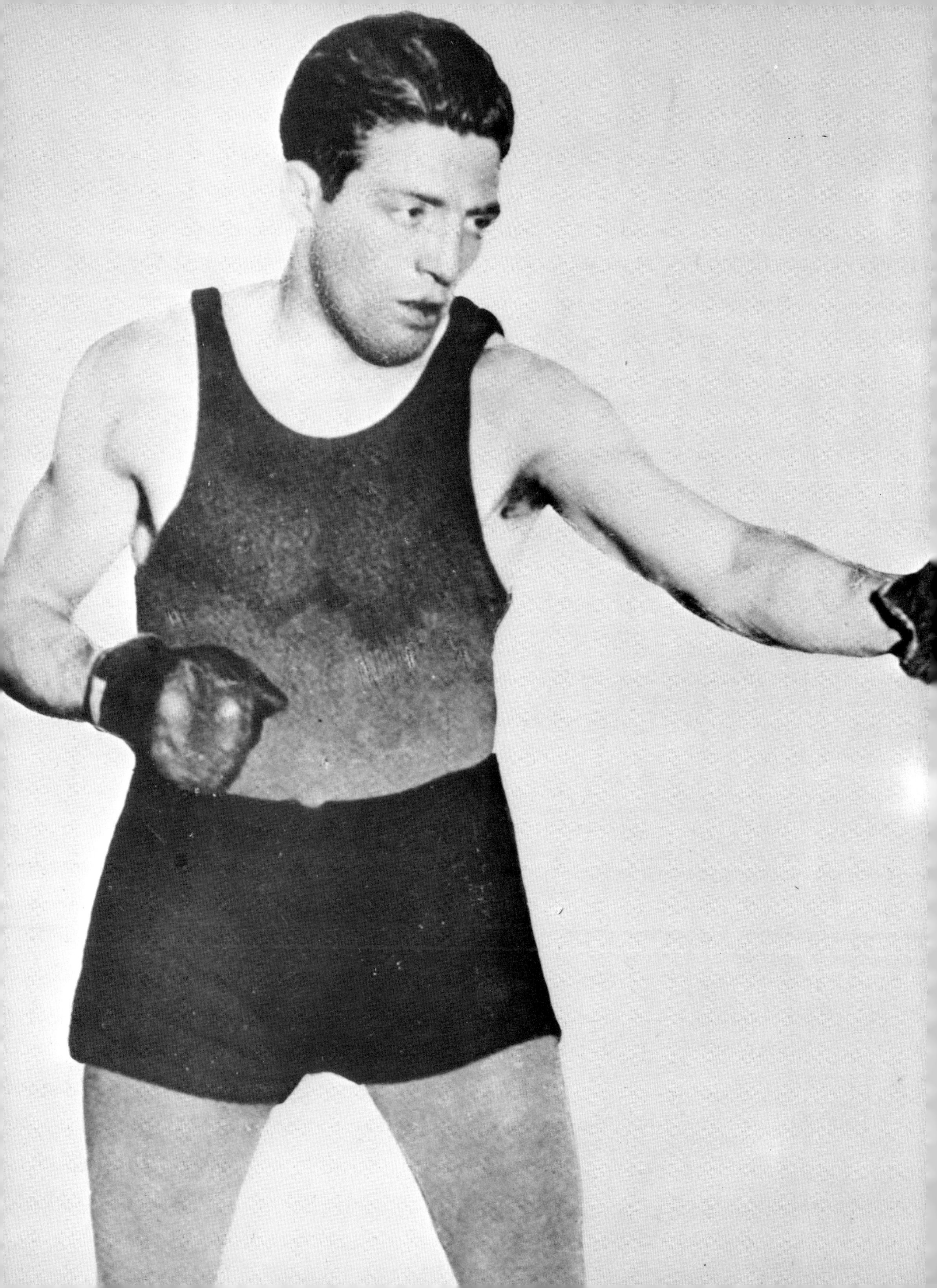

TED "KID" LEWIS

series of bouts with American welterweight Jack Britton. Lewis met Britton in the ring 20 times, winning three fights, losing four and drawing 13. In 1915 he defeated Britton to become World Welterweight Champion. Britton regained the title four years later.

In 1919 Lewis returned to England where he competed against the greatest fighters of his time, many of whom outweighed him. He knocked out Johnny Besham to become World Light Heavyweight Champion. After that he defeated Jack Bloomfield. One of his greatest fights was in 1922 against the famous French boxer, Georges Carpentier. Lewis relates:

> "For two minutes I chased Carpentier round the ring, and then the referee tried to stop the fight to say something. I let my arms down and Carpentier landed me a right to the chin. I went down and didn't manage to get up during the count, though I never lost consciousness."

Ted Lewis remained in the ring until December, 1929. After his retirement, he became a trainer, still devoted to the sport which brought him fame.

SIDNEY LUCKMAN
1916-

SIDNEY LUCKMAN

He was one of the most highly praised high school football players of all time. And with countless college scouts waving inducements in front of him, Sidney Luckman chose Columbia — and spent his whole college football career as a flashing diamond in a dull setting.

In his three years with the Lion eleven, the team won 10, lost 14 and tied 2. But Luckman was a player's player and a sportswriter's delight. So much so, that when Luckman failed to make any All-America team in his first year as a varsity player, N.Y. sportswriter Jimmy Cannon wrote a feature blasting those who made the selections.

From 1936 to 1938, with a weak line in front of him, Luckman passed and passed successfully in the face of charging opposition linemen. He tossed 376 passes in 24 games, completing 180 passes for 2,413 yards and 20 touchdowns — impressive figures for anybody on a mediocre team.

After Luckman was graduated, he had no intention of playing professional football. But George Halas, owner of the Chicago Bears, had followed Luckman's career closely and was determined to get Sid's name on a Bears' contract. He was convinced that Luckman was the man to play quarterback for the Bears in the new "T" formation. Perhaps the idea of being surrounded by the extra protection the "T" formation demanded for its quarterback — so different from his college football experience — convinced Luckman and he started with the Bears in 1939.

Luckman spent that year mastering the ins and outs of the tricky T formation with all its spins, pivots and precision ball handling. Then 1940 came and a shower of sparks hit the sports pages as the Bears won the Western Conference and the World Championship. The 1940 Championship game with the Washington Redskins was one for the books. After losing to the Redskins late in the season, the Bears clicked like a perfectly oiled precision instrument and blasted their opponents out of the stadium 73-0.

The next year, Luckman led the Bears to another champion-

Luckman blocks a pass intended for NFL All Stars' Merlyn Condit (1940)

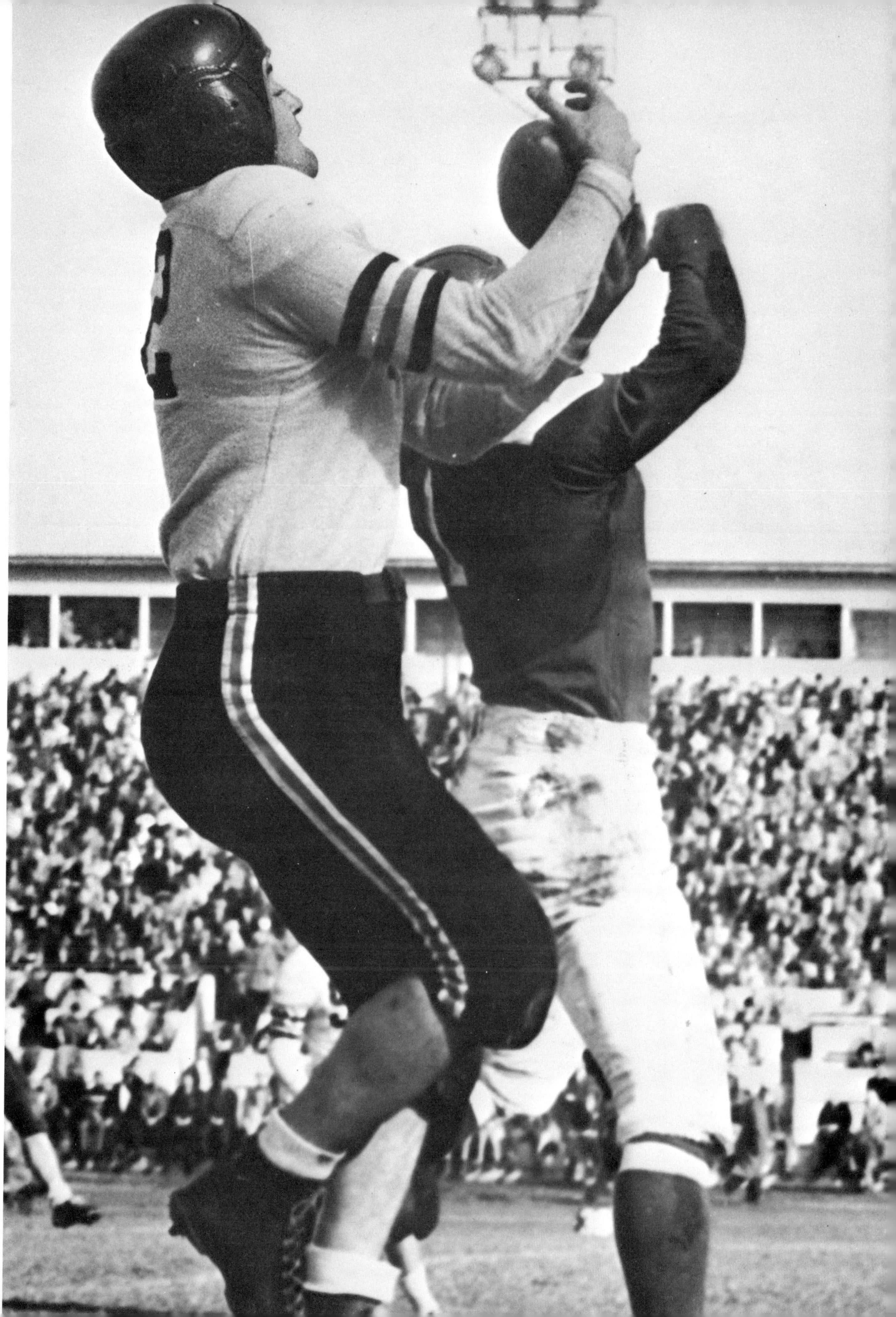

ship with a 34-9 win over the New York Giants, and in 1942 the Bears played a perfect season: 11-0-0. But they lost the big game and title to Washington 14-6.

But 1943 was the Luckman Year. Not only did he pace the Bears to another league title win. Not only did he personally bombard the Redskins in the title game to the tune of 41-21 with five touchdown passes. He also put on a midseason show at the Polo Grounds on Sid Luckman Day that will never be forgotten by any fan present.

He shot no less than seven touchdown passes into the air as the Bears smothered the Giants 56-7. He completed 23 out of 30 passes for 443 yards to establish a record.

In 1944 and 1945, the Bears' fortunes sagged. They finished second and fourth in the league standings. In 1946, Luckman pushed them to the heights again and in the championship game with the Giants, pulled a "Luckman special". With the score deadlocked at 14-14, he faked a handoff and carried the ball himself for the touchdown. The Bears won 21-14.

After Luckman closed his professional career in 1950, he coached Notre Dame, Columbia, Pittsburgh and Holy Cross in the mysterries of the T.

Luckman is currently in business in Chicago. He wrote *Luckman at Quarterback* and was elected to the Pro Football Hall of Fame in 1965.

ALLEN MAIMON
1920-

ALLEN MAIMON

In 1940, when Allen Maimon was a farmer in the Atlas Mountains of Algeria, he heard about field races being held at Algiers, and decided to participate. From that time on, he set his heart on track and field running, and kept in training for it.

Drafted into the French army in World War II, he first tried his skill at the 3000 meter run* and achieved a time of 9:20.0 minutes. After the fall of France, he served in the Free French Forces under General de Gaulle, and during the battle of Monte Cassino was wounded in the leg when his car drove over a land mine. After the war, he moved to Paris and began to train with the famous "Racing Club."

In 1946, Maimon won second place in the 10,000 meter French championship. He continued his training and won his first two French titles in two distances — 5000 meters and 10,000 meters. When France sent her best runners to Prague, Maimon was included. Prague was the home of one of the greatest long distance runners of all time, Emil Zatopek, known as the "Czech Locomotive." Maimon was still hardly a rival for the great Czechoslovakian. Zatopek beat him in the 5000 meter race by almost a complete lap.

From that time on, each time the two met, Zatopek held the upper hand. In the Olympic Games in London in 1948, Zatopek won the gold medal for the 10,000 meters, with Maimon in second place. Maimon did not despair. He continued training energetically, and in 1949 won the "Race of Nations" in England. A year later, he again competed against Zatopek in the European championship at Brussels and again had to be satisfied with second place.

In the Helsinki Olympic Games in 1952, Zatopek improved his performance. This time he swept the field with three gold medals — for the 5000 meters, the 10,000 meters, and the marathon. The duel between Maimon and Zatopek became legendary. Each time the "Czech Locomotive" won by a supreme effort only in the last few meters.

---

*1 meter = 3 feet, 3.28 inches

Illness forced Maimon to leave the course for two years, but in 1955 he returned to competition at the age of 35, suffering from violent attacks of rheumatism. In Belfast, Ireland, he again won the "Race of Nations" against English runners who had been certain of victory. Back in France, Maimon was awarded the cross of the French Legion of Honor.

In the 1956 Olympics, the great runners met once more, this time in Melbourne. Maimon was in fine condition, and in the preliminary race at Warsaw, had set a new record for the 10,000 meters: 20 minutes, 13.4 seconds. (Zatopek had won in the Helsinki Olympics in 1952 with a much slower time: 29:17.0) In Melbourne, it was predicted that the battle would again be between the Frenchman and the Czech. But a new star arose. A much younger man in superb condition, Russian Vladimir Kots, beat them both in the amazing time of 28:45.6.

Maimon and Zatopek were also entered in the marathon race. This proved to be Maimon's great day, for he ran a superb race. By the 25th kilometer,* he had left all his rivals behind him, and on the last seven kilometers, was out in front by more than half a kilometer. The perpetual runner-up at last became the winner — an Olympic champion, crowned with glory, the embodiment of every sportsman's dream. More than 100,000 people cheered him. Zatopek, who had fallen behind, finished in sixth place. Many experts have described Maimon's achievement as one of the most inspiring stories in the history of world sports — a lifetime goal achieved through iron will and determination.

*1 kilometer = six-tenths of a mile.

DANIEL MENDOZA
1764-1836

DANIEL MENDOZA

Daniel Mendoza, a young Portuguese Jew living in 18th-century England, was the first of his faith to become a champion boxer. He was also the father of the sport's scientific technique, and his fists helped dispel a vicious climate of anti-Semitism that prevailed in the British Isles at the time. Annals of the period describe the life of Mendoza and how for centuries Jews had been attacked on London's streets because people thought they would not fight back. From Mendoza's example, young Jews learned how to use their fists according to his rules, and could walk to and from their homes unafraid.

Mendoza's life as a young man was full of adventure. Once, during Purim, he dressed up as a sailor and was kidnapped and taken on board a ship. He left home in his early teens so as not to be a burden to his large family, and worked in a succession of London shops. Here, in extemporaneous street encounters, he soon became a local celebrity. The Prince of Wales, alarmed by the tide of anti-Semitic sentiment in England, heard of the young fighter and took a personal interest in his career in 1787. He arranged a match with one of the most prominent fighters of the time, Sam Martin, whom Mendoza defeated in 30 minutes.

Daniel was endowed not only with strength, but with intelligence. He saw boxing as an art requiring agility rather than brute force. At 21 he proudly announced the opening of his private boxing academy. He earned a good living and married a charming lady who, however, exacted a condition: that he concentrate on teaching. Daniel agreed, but he too made a condition: that she permit him to fight Richard Humphries, the uncrowned champion of England. Humphries had seen Mendoza fight several years before and had offered to train him. But a series of disagreements had turned the two men into bitter enemies.

The match, historians agree, stands as a landmark in sports history. There were no cameras at the time, but artists made sketches to show the course of the combat. Humphries dealt several vicious blows below the belt. Mendoza injured his ankle so severely

A contemporary artist depicts Mendoza in the "classical" boxing stance

that he could not remain on his feet. Humphries was proclaimed victor.

The next day Mendoza announced he wanted to fight a return match with Humphries, despite his injuries. While he recovered, both men published a series of letters in the newspapers, and the feud became a cause célèbre. Mendoza continued his training, and

119

supported himself with the income from his boxing academy. Finally the fight was scheduled for May, 1789. Such public interest was aroused that a special stadium was built. The French Revolution was a stirring topic of interest everywhere else, but in England men's thoughts were on the world's greatest prizefight. Mendoza won in 52 minutes and newspapers praised his agile style that countered the clumsy body thrusts of his opponent.

From this fight sportsmen concluded that brawn was less important to a boxer than training, technique, agility, timing, and lightness of movement. No longer would boxing be the sole province of musclemen; gentlemen from Eton and Cambridge would not be too proud to show their fists.

Mendoza was England's heavyweight champion from 1792-1795. Songs were composed in his honor, and portraits and medals made his face familiar to thousands. On the day the French populace stormed the Bastille, Mendoza published a booklet, *The Art of Boxing,* that created a greater sensation than the French news. A year later his old rival, Humphries, again challenged him and another match was arranged. The defeated Humphries had learned much from the Jew who had beaten him and now he employed the same tactics. The match was close. After a battle of 75 rounds that lasted one-and-a-quarter hours, Mendoza won. He remained champion until his defeat by John Jackson in 1795, at which time he announced that he would not again appear in public competition.

He did, however, fight in public again. He made a comeback in 1806, and again in 1820 at the age of 55. For a time, when he was forced to close his boxing academy, he gave exhibition matches in large London theater halls. Later his school was reopened and he devoted himself to teaching and writing his autobiography. He lived to a ripe old age that brought honor to the Jewish people, proud of a man who could give and take a punch in honorable combat.

WALTER MILLER
1890-

WALTER MILLER

Walter Miller was a jockey for only four years, but he rode 1094 winners. He was the first jockey to ride more than 300 winners in a season.

Yet at the peak of his spectacular career, Walter Miller vanished.

One day, when Walter was a teenager, his father took him to the track. From that day on, the boy's future was preordained. He was fascinated by what he had seen and began to visit Gravesend, Sheepshead Bay and Brighton Beach, where the Brooklyn tracks were. He had decided to become a jockey and nothing was going to stop him.

His father, a prosperous butcher, finally agreed not to stand in the boy's way and allowed him to start as an apprentice with a trainer.

Miller's first mount was a 3000-to-1 shot, which lost. But a couple of days later, Miller rode a 60-to-1 winner home and his short but spectacular career had its start.

In 1904, he went to California to ride for "Sunny Jim" Fitzsimmons. The boy was a natural athlete, the famous trainer recalled, and he never made the same mistake twice.

Walter came east again to ride under the colors of the James R. Keene Stable. And in 1906, this 98 pounds of determination made racing history.

This was the year he became the first man in history to ride more than 300 winners in a single year. In 1,384 races, he had 388 winners, 300 seconds, and 199 thirds.

And, in 1907, he repeated his triumph to win the national riding title again, with 334 wins in 1,194 races. And he made that incredible average again the following year.

Usually, Miller was assigned horses which were not very good, which makes his record even more remarkable. Walter Miller won the Futurity, Preakness, Saratoga Handicap, Travers and other racing classics.

However, Miller got too big. He grew to 5' 8 1/2" and 160

WALTER MILLER

pounds, so he went to Europe where he could ride at his increased weight.

He rode for the Kaiser and for Oppenheimer for whom he captured the Grand Prix of Berlin. Finally pounds took their toll and Walter Miller disappeared. He was spotted playing baseball in a small league in California, but disappeared again. It was generally thought he went to Paris to live, where it was said that he operated the Jockey Bar and owned a men's shop.

In 1945 he became seriously ill and needed surgery. Then came a mental breakdown from which he never recovered. He has spent the rest of his days in a mental hospital, reflecting, perhaps, on the short but glorious years when he wore the jockey's silks.

LIPMAN PIKE
1845–1893

LIPMAN PIKE

He was so fast that he once beat a horse for a purse of $200. He made $20 a week as America's first professional baseball player. He played on 16 different teams between the years 1865 and 1887. His name was Lipman Pike.

Pike's career was typical of precarious, rough-and-tumble professional baseball in the late 1800's. He changed teams almost yearly, saw clubs fold under his feet for lack of financial backing, and rose above the gambling interests that almost ruined the game. He managed to earn an honest living in the infant sport through sheer guts and ability.

Lipman Pike's parents left Holland and settled in Brooklyn, N.Y., when their five children were still young. Lipman and his brothers played the new game of baseball on what was then Long Island farmland, and in their teens became associated with various amateur baseball teams.

News of Lipman's speed and batting power as an off-and-on player for the Brooklyn Atlantics reached the Philadelphia Athletics in 1866. They offered him $20 a week to play third base for them. He stayed with the Athletics for a year, and became celebrated for his batting record, slamming six home runs in one game.

Then began a long and gypsy-like career. In 1867, at 22, he became player-manager of an Irvington, New Jersey club. He left it when Boss Tweed, owner of the Mutuals of New York, offered him a fat salary in the city. But he soon grew to dislike the Tweed management, and in 1868 returned to the Atlantics, by then the top team in the East.

In 1869, the first all-professional club was formed in Cincinnati. The Red Stockings swept the country for 130 straight wins, even defeating the formidable Atlantics. But in 1870, the Brooklyn team, with Pike at second base, finally stopped Cincinnati by a score of 8 to 7.

The National Association — the first professional baseball league — was born in 1871. It lasted only five years before being discredited by gambling, mismanagement and an ensuing lack of

LIPMAN PIKE

public support. Meanwhile, Pike was a member successively of the Troy Haymakers, the Lord Baltimores, the Hartford Nutmegs and the St. Louis Brown Stockings.

In 1876, the National League replaced the National Association. A year later, as player-manager of his old opponents, the Cincinnati Red Stockings, Pike became the League home run champion with *four home runs!* The ball the team was using was so dead that it seldom reached the outfield.

A baseball game of Pike's era, when bustles and top hats were proper grandstand attire and the players' dugout was a tent on the field

LIPMAN PIKE

In 1879, Pike left the reorganized Red Stockings to join a club in Springfield, Mass. Once again he was forced to look elsewhere as financial difficulties sank the team. In 1880, he hit another snag in Albany. Money troubles destroyed that club, too. Pike finally returned to New York City, and in 1881, after a short stay with his alma mater, the Atlantics of Brooklyn, he closed his career with a club in Worcester, Mass.

It was here that the only blemish appeared on an otherwise exemplary record. Pike was accused by the team management of intentionally booting a ball and (possibly in explanation for a poor Worcester showing) he was blacklisted for a year.

"Lip" went into the retail business and became a successful haberdasher in Brooklyn. He made a brief comeback with the original New York Mets in 1887, and umpired professionally for a few years thereafter. He died at the age of 48, surrounded by tributes to his career and character.

MYER PRINSTEIN
1880-1925

MYER PRINSTEIN

A blistering feud within the ranks of the U.S. Olympic track and field team probably resulted in some of the greatest jumping marks ever achieved in a short period of time.

The feud between Myer Prinstein of Syracuse University and Alvin Kraenzlein of the University of Pennsylvania peaked in the year 1899 and broke out in all its fury when they were Olympic teammates in Paris the following year.

The whole affair started because the American colleges sending men to the Olympics had agreed not to have their athletes compete on Sunday. On Saturday, Prinstein was leading in the trials with a jump of 23' 6 1/2". Then with the whole team resting, Kraenzlein jumped alone on Sunday, and won the gold medal by a half inch.

Prinstein immediately asked for a "jump off" on Monday but Kraenzlein would not agree. Although Prinstein was denied the gold medal he did take first prize in the triple jump, and a few days later, jumping in a meet in Paris, outdistanced Kraenzlein's Olympic mark with a leap of 23' 9 5/8".

Prinstein had begun to make a name for himself as a freshman at Syracuse where in 1898 he cracked the existing American and Intercollegiate longjump records with a leap of 23' 8 7/8". This was the first of a series of spectacular Prinstein wins until he bumped up against Patrick O'Connor who eclipsed Prinstein's best. But the next year at the Penn Relays, Prinstein came back to move ahead of O'Connor's mark with a jump of 24' 7 1/2. He also ran anchor man on the winning Syracuse mile relay team.

Although Prinstein was generally acknowledged to be the top American longjumper, he nearly missed the Olympics because Syracuse didn't have the funds to send him to Paris. A loyal alumnus had to step in and send him to Europe on one of his oil tankers or Prinstein never would have made it.

Prinstein entered as many competitions as often as possible, readying himself for the 1904 Olympics in St. Louis. There he secured titles in both the longjump and the triple jump, events in which he had missed four years earlier.

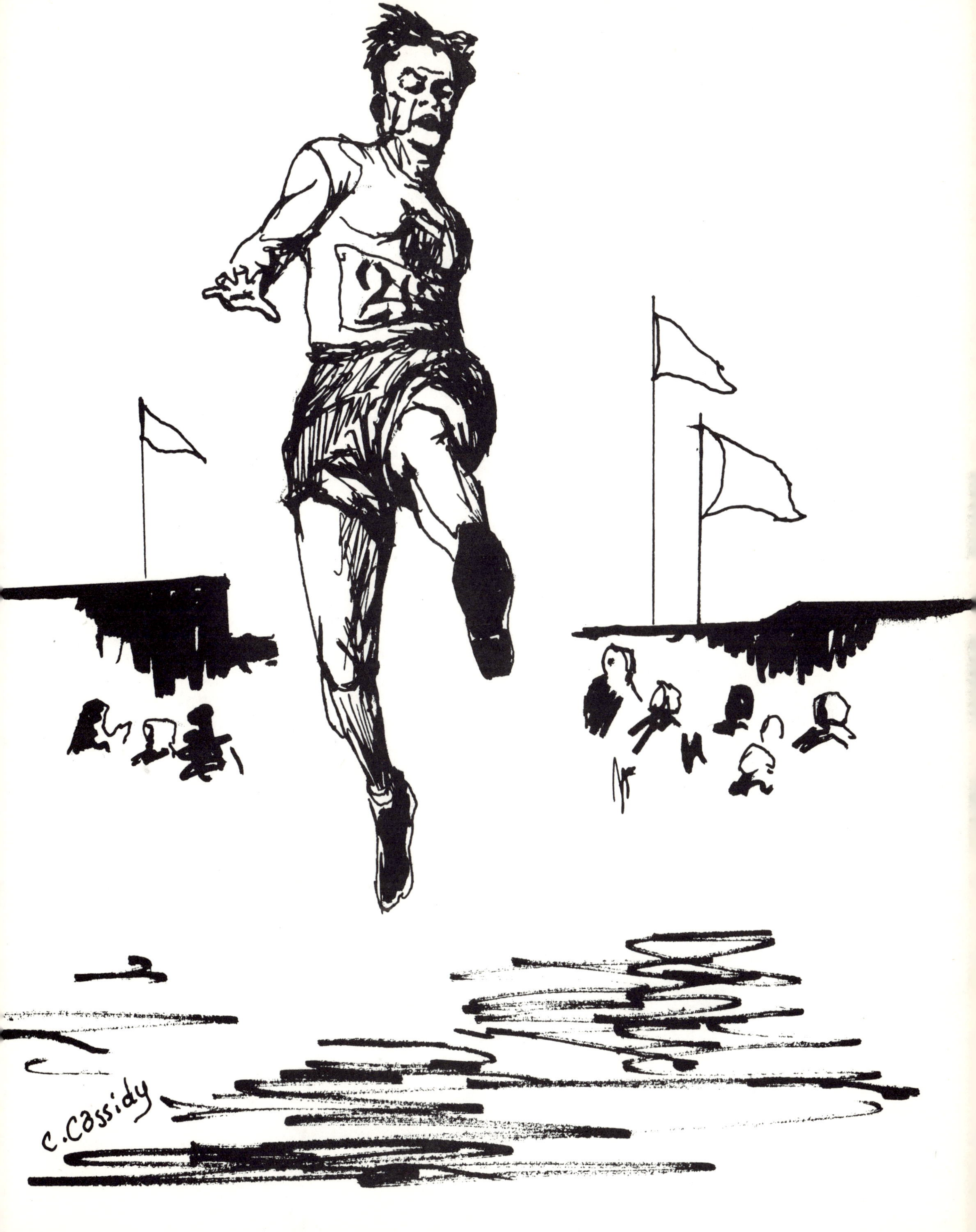
C. Cassidy

MYER PRINSTEIN

Although Prinstein had a victory-studded career, he hit snags a few times and in 1900 when he made his world record, there was not unanimous acceptance of his feat. Certain officials refused to accept the mark because of an aiding wind. Strangely, the mark stood as a world's record, but would not be accepted by the intercollegiate officials.

The secret of Prinstein's success? "His take-off," according to one of the top sportswriters of the day. "Prinstein doesn't hit the take-off board as fast as Kraenzlein but he gets more height."

Prinstein was graduated from Syracuse in 1901 and became a practicing attorney.

SAMUEL RESHEVSKY
1911-

SAMUEL RESHEVSKY

The eight-year-old boy had to stand on a chair to see the chess board properly. He made a move, climbed down, went to the next board. Spectators smiled at the display, but the chess players sitting opposite young Samuel Reshevsky had no time to appreciate the humor. They were too busy defending themelves, usually to no avail.

From his native Poland, through Germany, France and England, Samuel Reshevsky, the boy chess wonder, gave amazing exhibitions of simultaneous play, usually defeating 20 to 35 opponents in each match. During a week in New York after his European tour, Reshevsky defeated 19 West Point cadets without the loss of a game. In 1936, he won the title of United States Chess Champion, and kept it intermittently until the 1950's. He represented the United States in countless matches, and, while not always victorious, was deemed "the West's Number One player" by another world champion, a Russian.

Samuel Reshevsky was born to Orthodox Jewish parents in Ozorkow, in the Kalisz Province of Poland. He learned the elementary rules of chess when he was three years old, was able to defeat his father, who had taught him how to play, by the age of five, and was giving simultaneous exhibitions when he was six. The Polish Grand Master of chess Akiba Rubenstein predicted that the child would be chess champion of the world.

When the Reshevskys came to the United States, Samuel began his Jewish studies at the Yitzhak Elchanan Yeshiva in New York, and also had a tutor in English. The family moved to Detroit two years later. Here Samuel continued to improve his chess game, but received no formal education. A noted Jewish philanthropist, Julius Rosenwald (head of Sears, Roebuck & Co.) took an interest in the boy who repeatedly defeated him at chess. He convinced Samuel's family to settle down and give him a proper education. Rosenwald, together with the president of the Detroit Chess and Checker Club, Morris Steinberg, helped the Reshevsky family financially, and advised Samuel to drop chess while he completed his education.

Samuel made his mark in athletics on the Detroit High School

Reshevsky takes on 40 players from Yeshiva University simultaneously. He won 38, tied 2, lost none (1966)

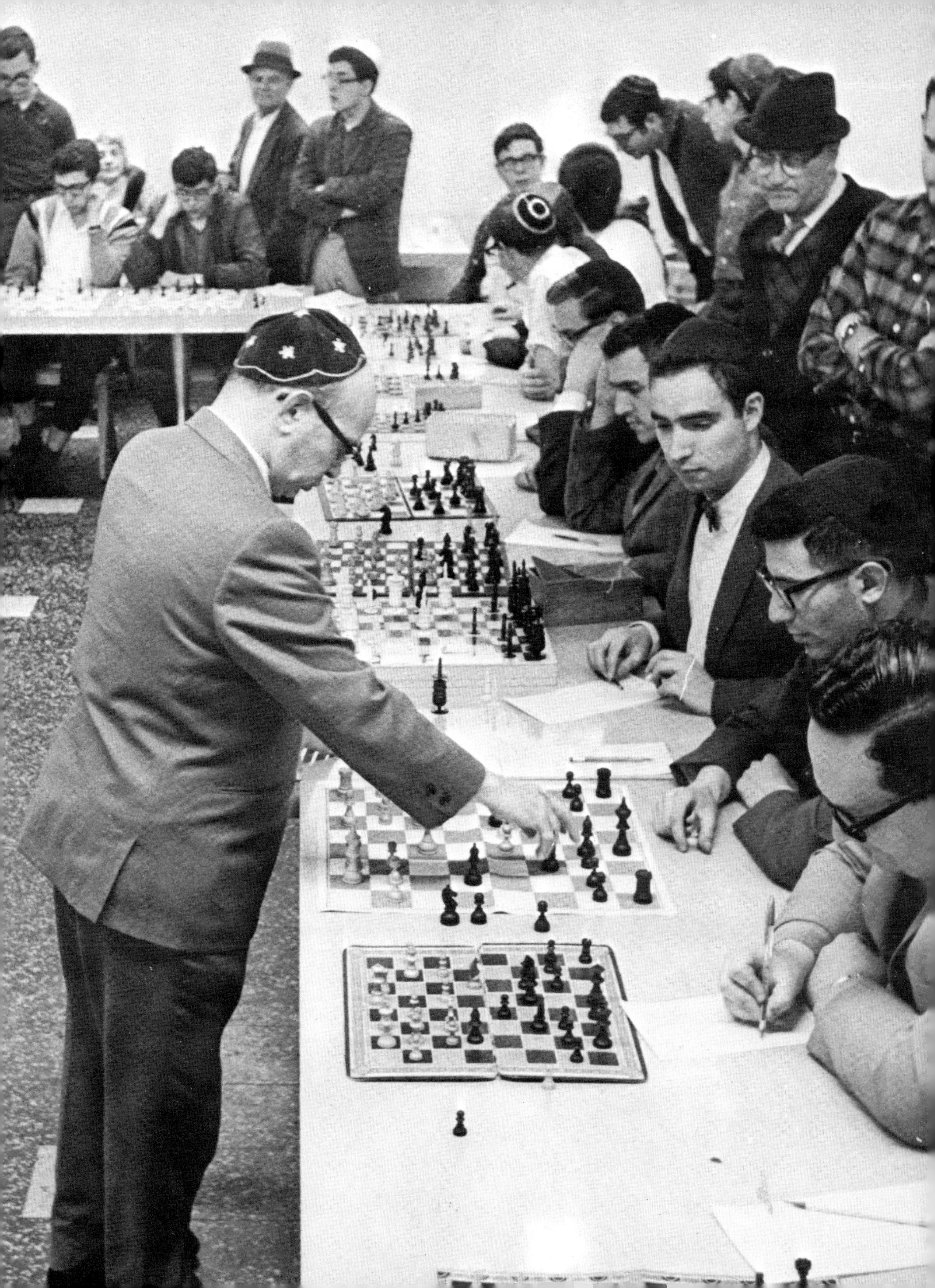

SAMUEL RESHEVSKY

baseball team, and was outstanding in mathematics at the University of Chicago. His grades in other studies were average. Only after he was graduated from college and had become an accountant did Reshevsky return to chess. Looking back at the lengthy break, he claimed that it had been good for him. Not only had he grown up like a normal boy, without the pressures of a child prodigy — he had matured, and his chess game was far superior to what it had been ten years earlier.

In 1931, against tough competition in the Western Chess Association in Tulsa, Oklahoma, Reshevsky took first place. He found little competition of his caliber in the United States, and in 1934 entered an international tournament in New York. Again, he took first place. Reshevsky's next big challenge was the United States Chess Championship which he won in 1936. During the following years, he won titles in tournaments in England, Latvia, and Sweden, and piloted an American team to four world championships and the Hamilton Russel Trophy, symbol of international team supremacy in chess.

Reshevsky's toughest competition came from Russian chess players. Russia now holds the Hamilton Russel Trophy, and also claims the Chess Champion of the World, Mikhail Botvinnik. Reshevsky led an American team against the Russians in two matches in 1946, and was defeated both times. Nevertheless, former World Chess Champion Vassily Smyslow stated that Reshevsky was the best player in the West.

Samuel Reshevsky has adhered to his religious upbringing throughout his career. He neither plays chess on the Sabbath nor eats food that is not kosher. When asked why he doesn't play on Saturdays even though his father thought it permissible, Reshevsky once answered: "To my father, chess was a game, a pleasure, a relaxation. To me it's a business, my livelihood." He carries kosher food supplies when traveling in case none is available in the area.

Reshevsky has not yet lived up to the prophecy of Polish Grand Master Rubenstein, but his career is far from over. He may yet earn the title of World Chess Champion. Many observers of the game believe that it is only a question of time.

MAURI ROSE
1906-

MAURI ROSE

Mauri Rose began his auto racing career on the dirt tracks around Dayton, Ohio, where he was born. The promise of gold on the California speedways lured him west. In 1934, he gained the spotlight at the classic Memorial Day 500 at Indianapolis by finishing second to Wild Bill Cummings in a disputed race. Two years later, although he came in fourth at Indianapolis, he was awarded the National Driving Championship.

In 1941, he finally crossed the Speedway finish line ahead of the pack. Rose won the 500 the second time in 1947 and repeated his victory in 1948. Of the two, the former race was packed with drama. It was the race in which Shorty Cantion was killed when he crashed into a wall at the southwest apron turn.

Newspaper reports called Rose's victory a spectacular triumph in which he "rallied from 14th place to battle for more than 100 miles with Lou Holland until eight laps from the end when he leaped into the lead to win by 32:12 seconds."

However, there was another story. Racing car owner Lou Moore, as was his custom, had entered two autos — one piloted by Rose, the other by rookie driver Bill Holland. With 25 miles to go until the flag waved down, the Moore cars were both out front with Holland in the lead. To guard against one or both of his cars being burned out as his drivers drove for the finish, Moore had the "EZY" sign flashed from the pit.

As Holland eased up, Rose kept on going to cross the finish line the winner.

When Holland reached the pit area, he was shocked to hear the result because he had thought he had won. Later, he ruefully admitted that he had lost count of the laps. However, Rose did it again in 1948 — becoming the third three-time winner of the Classic, with Wilbur Shaw and Lou Myers.

After a crash in 1951 from which he escaped unhurt, Rose retired from racing and now is employed by a major automobile manufacturer as an engineer.

BARNEY ROSS
1909-1967

Papa Rasofski, a little Talmudic scholar who had opened a grocery store in Chicago's ghetto, stood in his doorway waiting for customers. A man came in.

"Yes, please?"

"Empty out the cash drawer, quick!" The man held a gun, and was shaking with nervousness. Papa hesitated, thinking of his family. They had so little! A finger on the robber's impatient shaking hand jerked, and a bullet killed Papa Rasofski instantly.

Barnett Rasofski, 14 years old, took over the support of the family. His mother was sickly, and the Rasofskis were so poor that two of the boy's brothers and a younger sister were placed in an orphanage. Barnett worked at any odd job he could find — his only goal was to earn enough money to bring his family together again.

He decided to try his luck at amateur boxing in 1926, and a year later, won the New York-Chicago Intercity Golden Gloves featherweight championship. He turned professional in 1929, using an abbreviated form of his name — Barney Ross. Barney moved up in the ring rapidly, getting better-paid, more important fights each time. Finally, when he was 24 years old, he had a chance to fight in a championship bout, and won the world's lightweight boxing championship on his first try. The victory was more than a title — with family security assured, Barney reclaimed his brothers and sister from the orphanage.

Ross won the welterweight championship from Jimmy McLarnin in 1934, lost it in a re-match, regained it, and remained champion until 1938, during 17 subsequent fights. In the 18th, he was defeated by featherweight Henry Armstrong and retired from the ring. Ross was engaged to be married and was running a restaurant in Chicago, when his second career began. World War II was being fought against the cruellest enemy the Jews had ever faced.

Barney, although he was 33 years old, volunteered for the Marines. They turned him down. He used "pull," relying on people who had admired him during his golden days of boxing, to become accepted. He just had time to get married before being sent

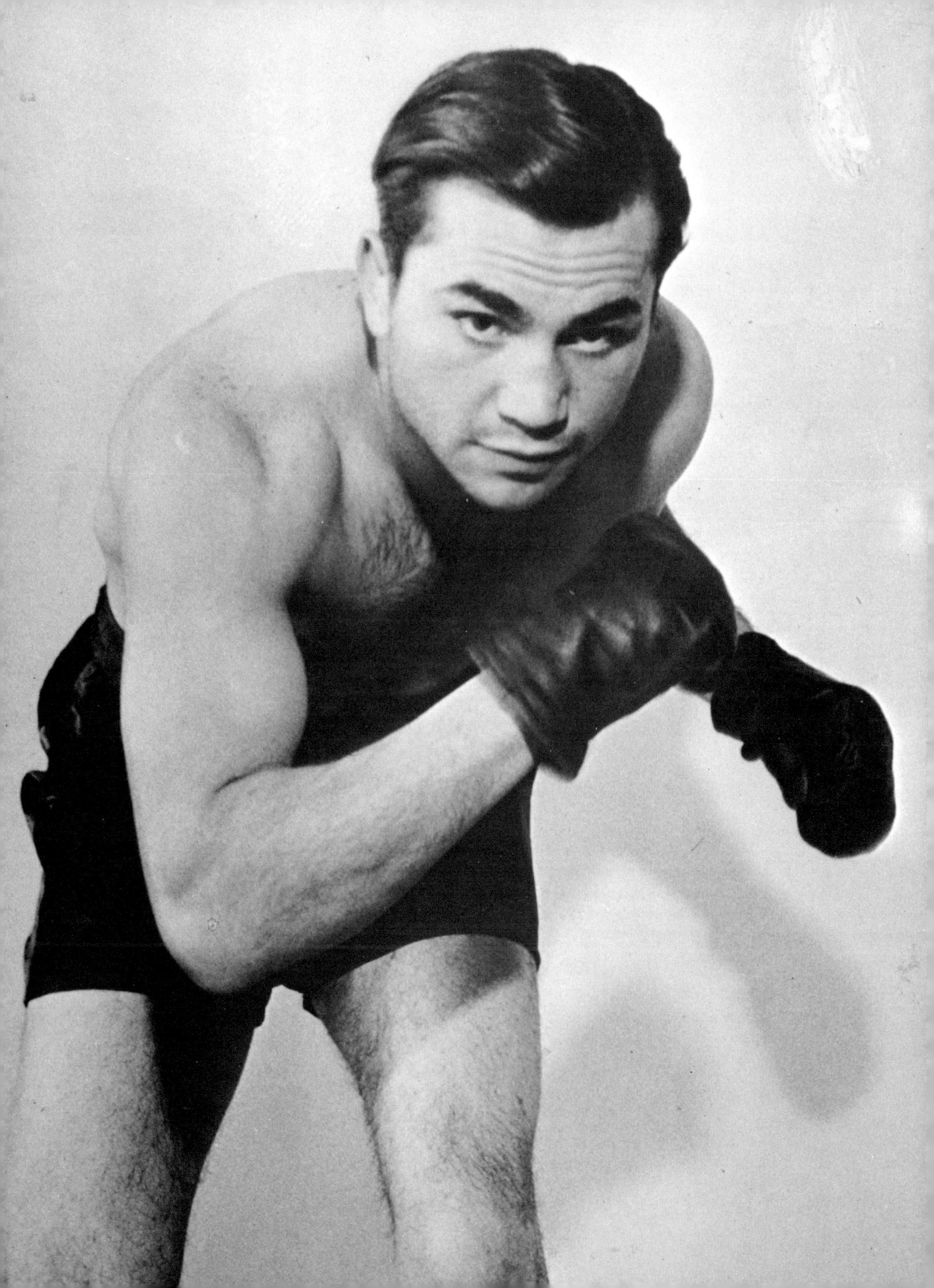

to Guadalcanal in 1942. The Japanese-held island had been attacked by the Americans a short time before. The Japanese were defending it fiercely, and Ross' unit was part of Marine reinforcements.

One of the men in Ross' squad was wounded immediately. As four Marines edged their way to safety with the wounded man, a Japanese machine-gun opened up, hitting everyone except Barney Ross, and killing the man the Marines were trying to save. Barney dug in to defend the wounded men. He dropped into a shell-hole and found two other wounded Americans there. Barney Ross began a single-handed defense of this position, which lasted for 13 hours. He used up all his bullets, then he used up all the other men's bullets. When he ran out of bullets, he began to throw grenades. When he was left with only one grenade, he fixed his bayonet in place on his rifle, and prepared to die.

During that long night, Barney was hit in his leg, hand and arm. He was also suffering from dizziness — his first in a long series of malaria attacks. He prayed, and the *Shema* was heard on Guadalcanal that night. When morning finally dawned, Barney was evacuated by a relief party who counted 22 dead Japanese around the shell hole.

Ross was a hero. He was promoted to corporal immediately and awarded the Silver Star and Distinguished Service Cross. The President of the United States wanted to present the medals to Barney in person, but the soldier's wife appeared in his place. Ross himself was too ill to accept the honors — his body was broken by malaria and his wounds, and his hair had turned white overnight

It took years for Barney Ross to regain his health. He became a drug addict, the victim of well-meaning medical corpsmen who had given him large doses of morphine to relieve his pain. This battle, and his eventual victory over drugs, were depicted in a film about his life, *Monkey on My Back,* and in his autobiography, *No Man Stands Alone.* Still a champion, Ross attributed this unusual achievement, and indeed all the successes throughout his life, to "a will to win" and to his strong commitment to the Jewish faith.

LOUIS RUBINSTEIN
1861-1931

LOUIS RUBINSTEIN

In January 1890, Canadian newspaper headlines read: "Rubinstein off to Russia" — and the sporting world waited in breathless excitement as the renowned Canadian figure skater sailed for Europe to compete in the International Championships at St. Petersburg.

Born in Montreal in 1861, Rubinstein was only 18 years old when he skated off with the Montreal figure skating title. In 1882 he became Canadian champion; three years later he was Champion of North America. He soon became known as the "father" of figure skating in the Western world.

When Rubinstein arrived in Czarist Russia, he encountered the most virulent anti-Semitism. First, he was summoned to police headquarters. A member of the skating committee accompanied him to explain that Rubinstein had come to Russia to compete in the international tournament. But the interpreter was ordered out of the room and a Russian police official proceeded to question the Canadian skater in English.

"You are a Jew?"

"Yes," Rubinstein replied, "and proud of it."

"And what is your purpose here in Russia?"

"You know as well as I," Rubinstein retorted. "I'm here as a sportsman to represent Canada."

The official dismissed him, but retained Rubinstein's passport.

For the next two days Rubinstein practiced for the tournament. On the second day, he was again summoned to police headquarters for more questioning. At the end of the interview, he was ordered to leave Russia within 24 hours.

Rubinstein appealed to Sir Robert Morier, the British Ambassador. Sir Robert declared that any British subject, Jew or Gentile, participating in an international sports competition would not be harassed or forced to leave the country. He promised to employ the British Embassy's influence at the Czar's court in Rubinstein's behalf.

Two more days passed. Rubinstein went on with his skating

practice. Then, at midnight of his third night in Russia, Rubinstein was routed from his bed and bustled off once more to the St. Petersburg Police Headquarters. Again he was questioned. Again he stated that he was in St. Petersburg to compete in the skating tournament, and he presented a letter of identification from the British Ambassador confirming the fact.

"Well, you of noble birth," said the Russian sarcastically, "you are obviously under honorable protection and I congratulate you on your good fortune. But let it be clearly understood, Mr. Rubinstein: You are to leave Russia immediately after the tournament." Then, taking Rubinstein's passport from his desk, the official crossed out the words "British Subject" — replacing them with the words, "L. Rubinstein, Jew."

"You do me great honor," Rubinstein said, as he retrieved the passport. "And I in turn will show you and all your bigots just what L. Rubinstein, Jew, can do!"

Rubinstein turned in brilliant performances in the figure skating contests of the next few days, winning medal after medal in competition against representatives of Austria, Norway, Finland, Sweden and Russia. A cable to the Montreal Gazette announced that the Canadian skater had defeated all competitors, but had been denied the championship because he was a Jew.

On the final day of the tournament, Rubinstein sat in a wooden shelter on the edge of the St. Petersburg outdoor skating rink. The next day he would leave the Czar's domain and be a free Canadian again. There was a knock on the door. In walked Sir Robert Morier, accompanied by the tournament judges.

"Well, Rubinstein," said the British Ambassador jovially, "I confess that I was beginning to doubt that you'd get a square show." And with this, each of the judges stepped forward to pin more medals on Rubinstein's jacket. He had won the world figure skating championship at last.

Rubinstein retired from competitive skating in 1891, after winning his last title in the United States Championships. The son of Polish immigrants, he became deeply involved in the civic affairs of his native city, serving as alderman, chairman of the first Montreal Athletic Commission, and president of the Montreal YMHA. He continued to be an influential figure in national and international skating associations, as well as a patron of, and participant in, other sports.

THE RUNNER OF AFEK
C. 1,000 B.C.

THE RUNNER OF AFEK

News of the Greek victory at Marathon in 490 B.C. had to be sent to Athens. It was 27 miles from the battleground to the capital, but a runner who had just returned from Sparta was dispatched. He covered the distance with inhuman speed, not stopping once. His lungs bursting, he was just able to gasp out the joyous news before he collapsed.

A similar race was run in Israel more than 500 years earlier. The Bible describes this historic event. We read in Samuel 1: "And there ran a man of Benjamin out of the army, and came to Shiloh the same day with his clothes rent and with earth upon his head." What was the important news that this "man of Benjamin" brought to Shiloh?

The battle between the Israelites and the Philistines was raging. The Philistines had concentrated their armies near Afek, and were preparing another attack. The Israelites had been defeated in their first encounter with the Philistines, and were in grave danger. It was decided to bring the Ark of the Tabernacle, containing the holy Torah, to the battlefield to raise the morale of the warriors, and in the hope that God would grant them victory.

The Ark was quickly brought and placed in the tent of Ebenezer, in the center of the encampment. But the Children of Israel were defeated a second time by the Philistines. An even greater catastrophe befell them: the Ark of the Tabernacle was captured by the enemy. It was imperative to notify the High Priest Eli, in Shiloh, of the loss of the Ark as quickly as possible.

At that time, strong and swift runners were given tremendous responsibility — they carried messages that meant life and death. And they had to pass through wild and unknown country with neither roads nor resting places.

A question now arises about the identity of this runner from Afek, who did not bring news of a victory, like the Marathon runner, but news of tragic defeat. Why did the Book of Samuel not give the name of the runner, but find it sufficient to say he was a

THE RUNNER OF AFEK

"man of Benjamin"? Many scholars believe this man to be Saul, the intended king of Israel.

Rabbi Levy and Rabbi Shimon, in the fourth century, argued about the distance the runner covered. Rabbi Levy claimed it was 60 parsah*; other scholars claimed it was 180. Although there was disagreement about the distance, there was unanimous accord about the identity of the runner: Saul. Why the controversy about the distance?

This third-century synagogue painting depicts the Philistines returning the Ark captured in the battle of Afek. They believed it brought them bad luck

THE RUNNER OF AFEK

Rabbi Levy held the opinion that the runner covered the distance between Afek and Shiloh only once; Rabbi Shimon believed that Saul was in Shiloh when the news reached him and that he rushed to Afek to witness the truth, then returned to Shiloh. Other authorities believed he covered the distance three times. Much has become legend, but even today scholars discuss the question. The Hebrew runner did not collapse like the runner of Marathon. Sages say that he was accompanied by the Angel of the Lord, who gave him the courage and strength to fulfill his mission.

*parsah—about 1 mile

DICK SAVITT
1927-

DICK SAVITT

In 1951, the year of the Davis Cup Finals between Australia and the United States, a meteor from America flashed across the courts in Australia. Dick Savitt won the Australian National Singles, singlehandedly walking through the whole Australian Davis Cup Team. Then he proceeded to England where he won the Wimbledon title in straight sets from Ken McGregor of Australia.

Yet Savitt was not considered good enough to play in the big matches for the United States Davis Cup Team! He was selected for the squad and played against Japan, but was left off the team in matches against Sweden and Australia. The United States subsequently lost the Davis Cup.

What happened? Was it really because Frank Shields, the American Davis Cup coach didn't like the way Savitt trained? Or was it because the strong Southern California tennis clique put the pressure on for Ted Schroeder, their native son? The real answer will probably never be known.

Dick Savitt, after this fantastic snub by his own country, proceeded to win the National Indoor Championship and then promptly announced his retirement from tournament tennis.

And in later years no matter how hard the officials of the United States Davis Cup Committee pleaded for him to make a comeback to help the United States regain its former tennis leadership, he consistently turned a deaf ear.

Dick had worked hard for his tennis triumphs. In his first two or three tournaments in 1947, he was eliminated quickly. But in 1950 he began to hit his stride and was ranked sixth nationally. In 1951 he was moved up to second place. And, of course, it was in 1951 that his famous Australian tour took place.

After the insult by the Davis Cup Committee, Savitt was not heard from, until the oil company he worked for transferred him to Texas. Then he played occasionally, but continued to turn down pleas by the American Davis Cup officials.

He was characterized as the one tennis player who came closest to Don Budge's style. In 1956 the American Davis Cup captain said

Savitt in action at Forest Hills, 1951

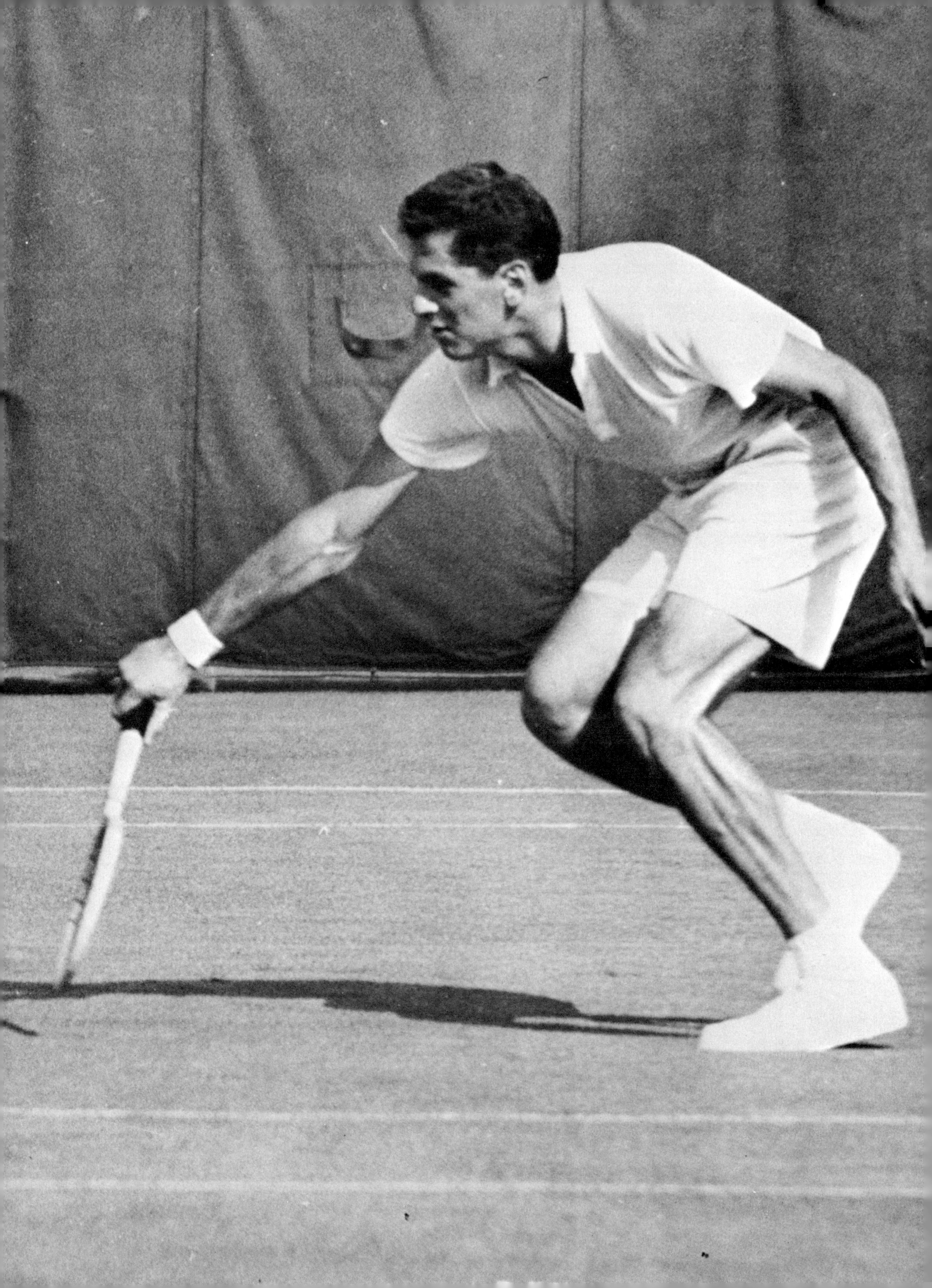

that Savitt had no equal in ground strokes, that he had one of the most potent services in the game and certainly would be a threat to any Australian. In that year, Savitt started playing in tournaments again. Though he was unofficially recognized as the No. 1 player in the country, he played in too few matches for his top ranking to be official.

He won the National Indoor Singles in 1958 and again in 1961, the first player to win it three times in 25 years. Also in 1961 he won the Maccabiah Games' singles and doubles crowns, ending his stormy but brilliant career on the courts. He is now an oil company executive.

ADOLPH SCHAYES
1928-

ADOLPH SCHAYES

Adolph Schayes has had one of the most incredible careers in basketball history. At one time he was holder of six records — most games played consecutively, most minutes played, most field goals made, most free throws made, most rebounds grabbed, and most points scored. On January 11, 1958, Schayes became the highest scoring player in professional basketball, with 11,770 points, surpassing the total of huge George Mikan.

Like many other of the "pro" basketball greats, he was underrated in his high school and college years. In fact, his coach at New York University excluded him from the All-Time NYU team. He was not, Howard Cann said, "particularly outstanding" while in college.

Schayes was graduated from NYU in 1948 and accepted an offer from Syracuse of the National Basketball League. He never doubted that he had made the right move, for here he came under the tutelage of Al Cervi, a great coach who shaped Schayes into the magnificent player he later became. The first year in Syracuse he was named Rookie of the Year.

In 1952, Schayes got an unusual break. He fractured his right wrist and with his right hand in a cast for a good part of the season, he had to learn to shoot with his left. The same thing happened in 1954. This time it was his left hand and the cast forced him to rest the ball on his fingers. The fingertip control he developed stood him in good stead for years.

In spite of the two injuries, Schayes played in 764 straight games from February 17, 1952, to December 27, 1961, when he collided with a Philadelphia player, shattering his cheekbone.

What made Schayes so great? For one thing, he was absolutely tireless. He averaged better than 18 points a game and physically drained his opponents. His incredible drive and stamina made him the fastest moving big man in the game.

One player who has been exposed to Schayes' pressure many times throughout the years, said: "With Schayes in the lineup, you never get any rest! He just keeps them coming at you."

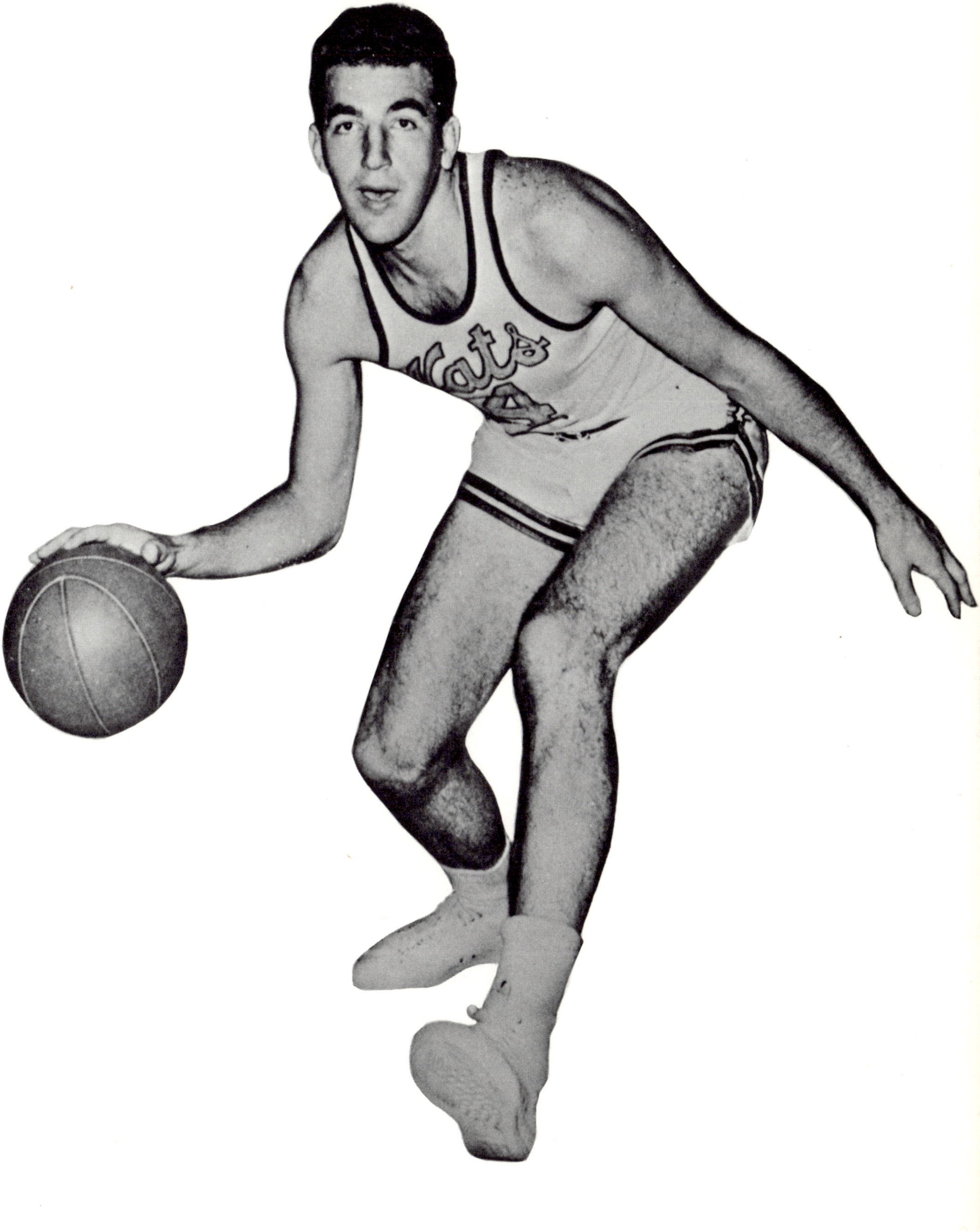

Schayes became a player-coach in 1964 when the Syracuse club moved to Philadelphia and changed its name to "The 76ers." In 1965 he became a full-time coach.

BARNEY SEDRAN
1891-

BARNEY SEDRAN

Barney Sedran was the tiniest man in the history of professional basketball. He stood 5'4" and weighed 118 pounds. But before he retired he was making more money than any other "pro" ball player — $12,000 a season, a far cry from his first salary of $200 a month. Nat Holman said in 1964: "Barney Sedran could do everything. A great outside and inside shooter, smart passer, and great ball handler, he was the most complete player of all time."

The son of Russian immigrants, Barney Sedransky was born in New York City. In describing his own childhood, he told why he thought so many boys brought up on the Lower East Side of New York gravitated to basketball instead of baseball. "There just was no room for baseball diamonds down there, but basketball was played in school houses, settlement houses and churches. For instance, I had four brothers and they were all good at basketball. It was the only sport we could play with little trouble."

Like many of the greats in basketball, it wasn't until Barney became a pro that he found himself. In high school he could not get a tryout for the team because of his height, and at the City College of New York he didn't really shine.

Basketball courts, in those days, were enclosed by "cages" made of chicken wire or rope. Teams carried eight men at most, and there were no substitutions. The ball was constantly in play because of the netting, and the game was fast and rough.

Of all his associations in pro basketball, Barney recalls the New York Whirlwinds most fondly: "I agree with all the experts who call it the greatest team of them all." There he played with Holman and Marty Friedman and the team, like the Original Celtics, was practically unbeatable. The Whirlwinds' final match, a three-game series with the Celtics in 1921, became the talk of the basketball world. The Whirlwinds won the first game 40-24, with Sedran scoring five goals before an audience of 11,000 people. They lost the second game 26-24. The third game never happened. Holman and Leonard, two of the Whirlwinds best men, jumped to the Celtics, and the Whirlwinds disbanded. Barney Sedran was elected

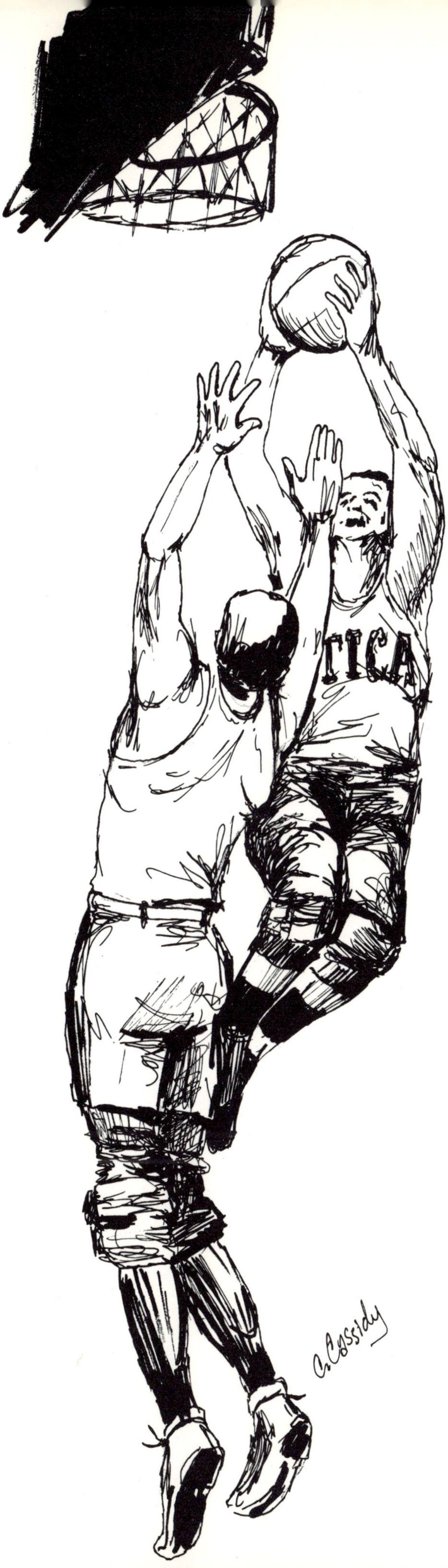
TICA

BARNEY SEDRAN

to the Basketball Hall of Fame in 1962, acknowledged by most experts as one of the finest basketball players of modern times. Characteristically, on receiving the honor, Sedran said he wished the Naismith committee had picked his friend Friedman — "the greatest basketball player I've ever seen."

SYLVIA WENE
1928-

SYLVIA WENE

In 1945, at a Philadelphia bowling alley, petite Sylvia Wene, age 17, stared with open mouth and sparkling eyes at the world which would one day draw her into its special excitement and be the dominating influence in her life.

This 4'11", 128-pound girl, who was denied the fun of bowling that first night because she was too short, was to prove in just a few years that a woman could bowl as well as a man — and she proved it in the white heat of competition.

The world of gleaming alleys and clashing pins fascinated her and she devoted herself to the sport. Although she took care of the family grocery business during the day, she practiced bowling every night she could. "To get on top and to stay there," said Sylvia, "you really have to practice every single day and to play in competitions. I play in three different leagues every week. I average between 35 and 40 games a week. I'm much more active than I was as a teenager. I used to be an ardent spectator of baseball and that was it."

On March 28, 1951, she bowled a perfect game. The bowling fraternity knew a star had been born. It was the first 300 ever rolled by a woman on the East Coast. When Sylvia first made tenpin headlines, she was nicknamed "Butterball." When she joined the bowling promotion staff of AMF, a manufacturer of bowling equipment, the firm had trouble dressing her properly because of her rolypoly figure. AMF had her dresses specially designed to make her look slimmer. It didn't help. So she helped herself by losing the weight.

Her second perfect game was rolled in the final of the World's Invitational Match Game Tournament on December 11, 1959 — the only 300 game ever recorded by a woman in match play.

Less than a month later, she rolled another perfect score in the All Star Tournament, which she won — another first for Sylvia, for no other woman had ever rolled 300 in the history of this tournament.

Sylvia Wene is the only woman who has ever rolled more than

January 15, 1960: Sylvia Wene shares a happy moment with Harry Smith, as winners of the women's and men's championships at the All-Star Bowling Tournament in Omaha

1960 MEN'S
NATIONAL INDIVIDUAL
ATCH-GAME CHAMPIONSHIP
WON BY
1960 WOMEN'S
NATIONAL INDIVIDUAL
MATCH-GAME CHAMPIONSHIP
WON BY

SYLVIA WENE

one accredited 300 score. In addition she has rolled 297 twice and 288 four times. In 1961 she personally proved the point that women could bowl as well as men when she rolled a four-game series of 930 to blanket a field of outstanding men competitors in the Penn Recreational National Open.

When she and Adele Isphodring won the Women's International Bowling Congress doubles crown they missed the all-time record of 1,264 by one pin! Sylvia's score — 673; her partner's — 590.

Sylvia Wene established the all-time high of 206 league average during the seasons from 1952 to 1955. She hit the first of her dozen "700" series in 1951. And six of the "700's" were recorded during one season — a precedent-smashing achievement. In 1955 and 1960 Sylvia Wene was the Woman Bowler of the Year. She was a member of All America Teams in 1955 and from 1959 through 1962 and captain of the All America Team in 1960.

Between her duties at AMF and her startling performances in bowling competitions, Sylvia enjoys roller skating and playing the accordion. The grocery store? She sold that in 1955.

HENRY WITTENBERG
1918-

HENRY WITTENBERG

"Henry, Jewish boys don't fight. It's not nice."

"Sorry, Papa. But he started it."

"And you finished it, I notice. Now I'll have to apologize to the boy's family. But he's older than you. How...?"

Henry Wittenberg has been called the world's greatest wrestler — amateur or professional. Sports have dominated his life — as U.S. Amateur Wrestling Champion, as an Olympic gold and silver medalist, as holder of eight national free-style titles at his retirement in 1953, and throughout his career in the New York City Police Department, as a coach in various youth programs.

Amateur and professional wrestling are quite different. Professional wrestlers — who get paid for their appearances — are really actors. The terrifying blows they give and receive are faked. TV wrestlers spend hours practicing with each other to simulate ferocity and mayhem, but the contest is not real sport. There are no "bad guys" and "good guys" in honest athletics.

Wittenberg, an amateur who loved the sport, once published a challenge to any professional wrestler who would fight him. Wittenberg bet $5,000 (which if he won would go to charity) that he could pin down any professional in 30 seconds. There wasn't a single professional "grunt-and-groaner" willing to take him up on the bet.

Amateur wrestling is a test of skill, strength, and agility. The contestants start with a special grip. The two men move like cats, using science and strength. There are rules and points, and, finally the pinning of one contestant to the floor. Blows or grips that might lead to serious injury are prohibited.

Henry began wrestling when he was a student at City College of New York. By the time he was graduated in 1939, he was runner-up in the NCAA championships. He did not lose a match again until 1952. After becoming the U.S. Amateur Champion, he went to the Olympics in London in 1948. He won a match with a Finn on points. He pinned an English wrestler in 47 seconds. A Hungarian lasted two minutes and 20 seconds. A Swedish wrestler succumbed next. The final match pitted Henry against another Swede, Stekli, and is still remembered as a classic. Wittenberg won and

A 1946 team photo with Wittenberg at right

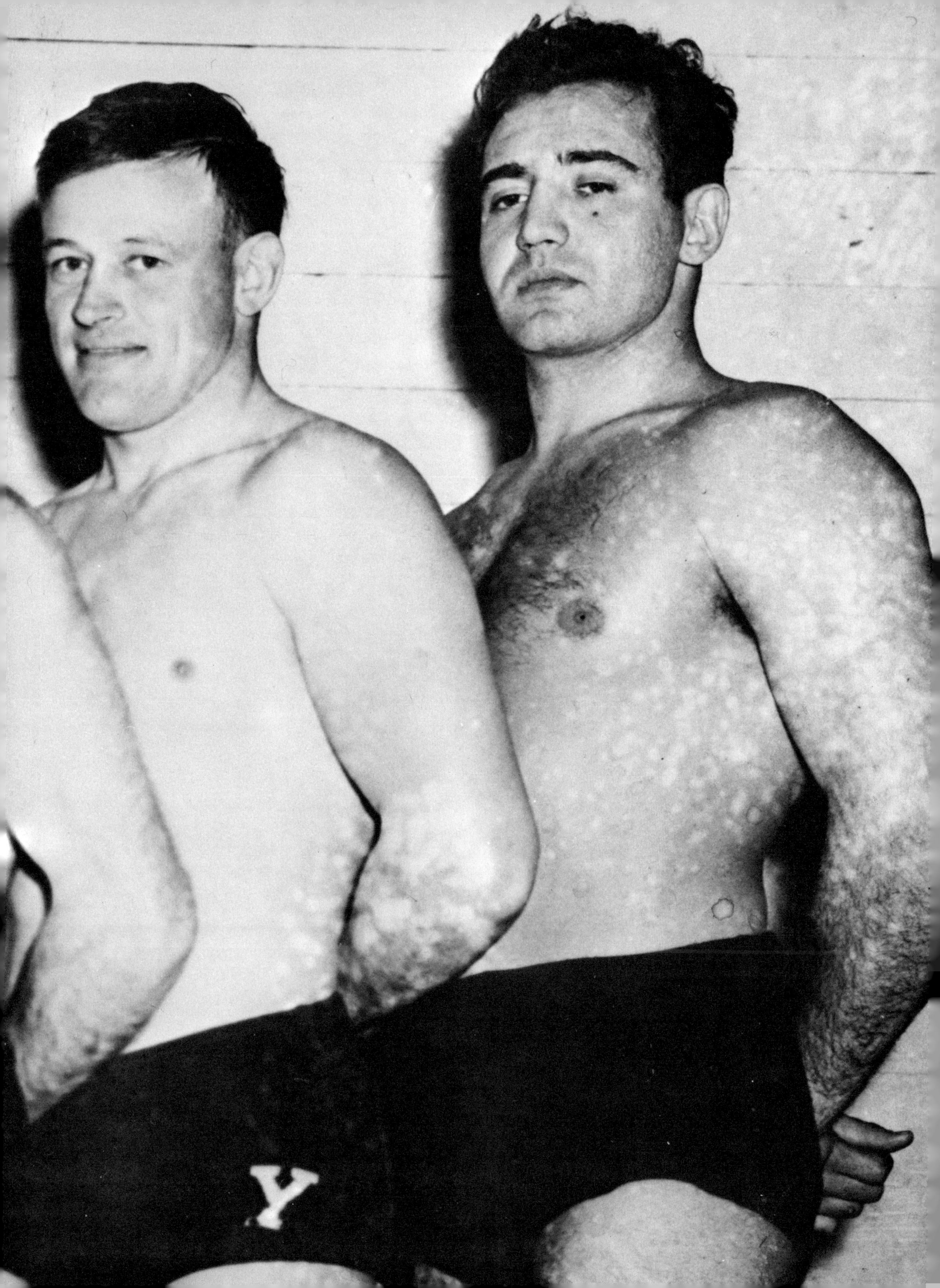
Y

HENRY WITTENBERG

was named light-heavyweight Gold Medal Champion of the Olympics.

Henry Wittenberg is not the only Jewish champion in wrestling. In almost every Olympiad a Jew has won an important place in the wrestling competition. In 1908, Ricard Weiss, Hungarian wrestling champion, won the heavyweight gold medal. Another Jew, Tybor Fischer, followed Weiss to become Hungarian champion in 1910, and later champion of the world. In 1920, at Antwerp, American Jew Samuel Gerson took a silver medal. In 1928, another American Jewish athlete, Eli Morrison, won the Olympic gold medal in the featherweight free-style division. In 1932 Hungary's Karely Karpati won the free-style lightweight silver medal, and Abraham Kelard of Denmark won a silver medal in Greco-Roman wrestling. In 1936, Karpati took a first place in the Berlin Olympics.

Wittenberg took part in the Maccabiah, the Jewish international sports competition in Israel. Here the American and Olympic champ became Maccabiah champion, too. Wittenberg later became interested in Zionist activities, and toured with a film of the Maccabiah for the benefit of the United Jewish Appeal.

Being human, Henry Wittenberg also lost. At the 1952 Olympics in Helsinki he was ill but nevertheless defended his title. In his first match with an athlete from Venezuela, Henry won in one minute, 28 seconds. He pinned his next opponent, from Switzerland, in less than one minute. But the next contender, a Swede named Falm, won on points after a tough match. With great effort, Wittenberg defeated his last two opponents on points. The single loss to the Swede cost him the gold medal and he received the silver medal instead.

Back in the United States Wittenberg again won the American championship and kept the title for many years. During his long, outstanding career, he spent two years in the U.S. Navy, obtained a Master's degree from Columbia University, and won five Police Department citations for bravery. He is author of a book, *Isometrics*. Wittenberg's wife is a former policewoman; his son shares his father's interest in wrestling, being the winner of two Maccabiah gold medals himself.

INDEX

Abrahams, Harold, 11 ff
American League, 40, 60
AMF, 164, 166
Anti-Semitism, 118
Armstrong, Henry, 140
Art Of Boxing, The, 120
Athletics, Philadelphia, 88, 126
Atlantics of Brooklyn, 128
Attell, Abraham, 15 ff
Auerbach, Arnold, 19 ff
Australian National Singles, 152
Auto Racing, 138

Bapte, Norval, 74
Barna, Victor, 23 ff
Baseball, 40, 58, 86, 90, 126
Basketball, 20, 34, 66, 156, 160
Basketball, Hall Of Fame, 162
Berger, Isaac, 27 ff
Bieber, Isadore, 70
Blum, Walter, 29 ff
Boston Braves, 88
Boston Celtics, 20, 21, 66, 160
Botvinnik, Mikjail, 136
Bowling, 164
Boxing, 16, 36, 106, 118, 140
Boykoff, Harry, 33 ff
Brandeis University, 54
Braves, Boston, 88
Britton, Jack, 108
Brooklyn Atlantics, 126
Brooklyn Dodgers (Football), 54
Brown Stockings, St. Louis, 127
Bullfighting, 48

Cantion, Shorty, 138
Cardinals, St. Louis (Football), 56
Carpentier, Georges, 108
Celtics, Boston, 20, 21, 66, 160
Cervi, Al, 156
Chance, Frank, 86

Chess, 44, 94
Chess and Checker Club, Detroit, 134
Chess Association, Western, 136
Chess Championship, U. S., 136
Chicago Bears, 110
Chicago Cubs, 86
Chicago White Sox, 86
Choynski, Joe, 35 ff
Cincinatti Red Stockings, 88, 126, 127
Cincinatti, University of, 90
City College of New York, 34, 54, 66, 168
Cleveland Indians (Football), 53
Cobb, Ty, 86
Colonels, Louisville, 40
Columbia University, 48, 110, 112, 170
Corbett, Jim, 36
Cousy, Bob, 20
Cummings, Wild Bill, 138

Davis Cup, 152
Dempsey, Jack, 104
Detroit Tigers, 58, 60
Detroit Wolverines, 54
Dodgers, Los Angeles, 90
Dreyfuss, Barney, 39 ff

Fencing, 78
Fischer, Bobby, 43 ff
Fischer, Tybor, 170
Fitzsimmons, Bob, 37
Fitzsimmons, "Sunny Jim", 122
Football, 52, 56, 82, 110
Forbes Field, 41
Fordham University, 56
Forest Hills, 98
Franklin, Sidney, 47 ff
Friedman, Benny, 51 ff
Friedman, Marty, 66, 160
Futurity, The, 122

Giants, N. Y. (Baseball), 74, 86
Giants, N. Y. (Football), 53, 54

Goldberg, Marshall, 55 ff
Golden Gloves, 140
Grange, Red, 52
Greenberg, Hank, 57 ff, 90

Hajos, Alfred, 61 ff
Hartford Nutmegs, 127
Hemingway, Ernest, 50
Hodesblatt, Max, 34
Holland, Bill, 138
Holland, Lou, 138
Holman, Nat, 65 ff, 160
Holy Cross, 112
Horse Racing, 30, 70, 122
Humphries, Richard, 118-120

Ice Skating, 74, 144
Ice Skating, St. Petersburg International
  Championships, 144
Indianapolis, Memorial Day 500, 138
Israel, 68, 170

Jackson, John, 120
Jacobs, Hirsch, 30, 69 ff
Jaffee, Irping, 73 ff
Jeffries, Jim, 38
Johnson, Jack, 37

Kabos, Endre, 77 ff
Kansas City Blues, 88
Karpati, Karely, 170
Kelard, Abraham, 170
King, Philip, 81 ff
Kling, John, 85 ff
Kots, Vladimir, 116
Koufax, Sandy, 89 ff
Kraenzlein, Alvin, 130

Lasker, Emanuel, 93 ff
Lenglen, Suzanne, 97 ff
Leonard, Benny, 101 ff, 106

Lewis, Ted "Kid", 105 ff
Little, George, 52
Lord Baltimores, 127
Los Angeles Dodgers, 90
Louisville Colonels, 40
Luckman, Sidney, 109 ff

Maccabiah Games, 170
Maimon, Allen, 113 ff
Marathon, 148, 150
Mathewson, Christy, 92
McLarnin, Jimmy, 140
Mendoza, Daniel, 106, 117 ff
Michigan, University of, 52
Michigan Wolverines (Football), 52
Mikan, George, 156
Miller, Walter, 121 ff
Monkey On My Back, 142
Morrison, Eli, 170
Myers, Lou, 138

National Basketball League, 156
National Indoor Tennis Championship, 152
National League, 40, 86, 90, 92, 127
Navy, 53
NCCA, 168
New York Giants (Baseball), 74, 86
New York Giants (Football), 53, 54
New York, Mutuals of, 126
New York University, 156
New York Whirlwinds, 66, 160
New York Yankees, 40, 188
No Man Stands Alone, 142
Northwestern University, 52
Notre Dame, 54, 56, 112

O'Connor, Patrick, 130
Ohio State, 53
Olympic Games, 12, 62, 76; Antwerp, 12;
  Berlin, 78; Helsinki, 110, 115, 170;
  London, 114, 168; Melbourne, 28;
  Paris, 28, 130; Tokyo, 28

Philadelphia Athletics, 88, 126
Pike, Lipman, 125 ff
Ping-Pong, 24
Pittsburgh Pirates, 40, 56, 60, 112
Preakness, The, 122
Princeton Tigers, 82
Princeton University, 82
Prinstein, Myer, 129 ff

Race of Nations, 114
Racing Club, 114
Reshevsky, Samuel, 46, 133 ff
Rice, Grantland, 52
Rockne, Knute, 52, 54
Roosevelt, Theodore, 48
Rose, Mauri, 137 ff
Rosh Hashanah, 58
Ross, Barney, 106, 139 ff
Rubinstein, Louis, 143 ff
Runner of Afek, The, 147 ff
Runyon, Damon, 17
Russel, Hamilton Trophy, 136
Russell, Bill, 20, 21

Santa Anita, 32
Saratoga Handicap, 122
Savitt, Dick, 151 ff
Schayes, Adolph, 155 ff
Schroeder, Ted, 152
Sedran, Barney, 66, 159 ff
Seventy-Sixers, The, 158
Seville, 48, 50
Shaw, Wilbur, 138
Silver Skates, 74
Smith, Harry, 164
Smyslow, Vassily, 136
Soccer, 24, 66
Sparta, 148

Suffolk Downs, 70
St. John's University, 34
St. Louis Brown Stockings, 127
St. Louis Cardinals (Football), 56
Steinberg, Morris, 134
Steinitz, William, 94
Swimming, 62
Syracuse University, 130

Table Tennis, 24
Tennis, 98, 152
Texas League, 86
Tigers, Princeton, 82
Tinker, Joe, 86, 88
Track, 12, 130, 114
Travers, 122
Troy Haymakers, The, 127

United Jewish Appeal, The, 170
United States Davis Cup Team, 152

Waddell, Rube, 40
Wagner, Honus, 40
Washington, George University, 22
Weightlifting, 28
Wene, Sylvia, 163 ff
Western League, 86
Wimbledon, 98, 100, 152
Wisconsin, University of, 83, 84
Wittenberg, Henry, 167 ff
Wolverines, Michigan (Football), 52
World Series, The, 40, 41
Wrestling, 168

Yale University, 54
Yom Kippur, 59, 60, 90
Zatopek, Emil, 114

GENERAL INDEX

This is a complete index of subjects covered in Volume I through X. Boldface entries indicate a full biography for the subject.

A

Aaron, II:256
Abba Arikha (Rab), I:142
Abd el Kadr Husseini, II:398
Abelard, Peter, II:179
Abell, Nils H., V:56
Abelson, Dr. Phil, V:102
Abijam, I:38
Abimelech, I:30, 32; VII: 70
Abraham, I:12, 15, 26
Abrahams, Harold, X:11 ff
Abravanel, Don Isaac, VIII:11 ff
Absalom, I:35; VII:46; monument of, I:81, 88
Abu Al-Kasim Ibn al'-Arif, VIII:84
Abu Agheila, II:338
Academy Award, VI:42, 132
Acetyl co-enzyme, IV:82
Acetyl phosphate, IV:102
Achad Ha'am, II:238, 239; IX:11 ff, 90
Achdut Ha-Avodah (Labor Zionist Party), VII:14; VIII:40
Acre, I:84
Actors, VI:12, 90, 130, 150, 173
Actresses, VI:26, 42, 160, 182
Adadnirari III, I:40
Adiabene kings, I:107
Adler, Marcus Nathan, V:17
Adonijah, VII:46
Adrenal cortex, IV:142
Adrenalin, IV:108
Adrenosterone, IV:142
Advisory Council on the Arts of the State Department, VI:144
Aelia Capitolina, I:127; VII:32
After the Fall, VI:127
Agadah, I:124, 136; IX:52
Agricultural Advisory Commission, VIII:134
Agrippa I, I:105, 106
"*Agunot*" (Deserted Women), IV:12
Ahab, I:38, 39, 40
Ahaz, I:40, 54, 58
Ahaziah, I:40, 49
Ahijah, I:37
Ahiyo, I:79
Ai, VII:80
Akhenaton, I:16, 25
Akiba, Rabbi, I:128; VII:30, 32
Alamogordo, IV:54
Albumin, IV:90
Alcoves, Les, VI:134
Aleichem, Shalom, II:219; IX:15 ff
Alexander Jannaeus, I:87, 99, 100, 102
Alexander (son of Miriam, the Hasmonean), I:105
Alexander the Great, I:79, 82, 83
Alexander II, of Russia, II:210
Alexandria, I:84, 87, 108, 141
Al Fatah ("Conquest"), II:330
Algebra, V:60
Algebraic Numbers, V:61
Algeria, II:334, 337
Al Hakim, Caliph, I:146, 147; VIII:174
Alhambra Palace, VIII:85
Aliyah, II:238, 239, 255, 279, 281, 282, 286, 307, 308, 311
Alkalis, V:90
Allegro, VI:67
Allen, Fred, VI:18
Allergies, V:118
Alliance Israelite Universelle, II:218; VIII:56
All My Sons, VI:127
Allon, Yigal, VII:11 ff, 136
Almoahids, I:148
Alroy, David, VII:15 ff
Alsace, II:207
Alternating current, V:139
Altneuland (Old-Newland), VIII:88, 92
Altneu Schul, II:193, 213
Altona, II:208
Always You, VI:66
Amalekites, VII:68
Amaziah, I:49
Amenophis III, I:16
Amer, Abdel Hakim, II:332, 343
America (see also United States), II:180, 191, 192

America-Israel Cultural Foundation, VI:180; VIII:106
America Symphony, VI:40
American Democracy, The, VIII:108, 110
American in Paris, An, VI:58
American Institute of Electrical Engineers, V:136
American Jewish Committee, II:252
American Joint Distribution Committee, VIII:118
American League, X:40, 60
American Presidency, The, VIII:110
American Society of Composers, Authors and Publishers, VI:98
American Society of Plant Physiologists, IV:60
Amman, II:337
Ammon, Ammonites, I:30, 35, 36, 40, 49, 75; VII:76, 78
Ammonia gas, IV:70
Amorites, I:27, 28, 29
Amos, I:51
Ampere, V:12
Amsterdam, II:191, 195, 203, 212
Amsterdam Art Academy, III:62
Anan ben David, II:178
Anatomy V:142
Anderson, Karl B., IV:150
And So It Came To Pass, IX:52
Anilewicz, Mordechai, VII:19 ff
Annie Get Your Gun, VI:67
Anthrax, V:29
Antibodies, IV:44
Anti-Defamation League, II:252
Antigonus, I:87, 104
Antioch, I:108, 141
Antiochus III, I:83
Antiochus IV (Epiphanes), I:84-88, 97, 98; VII:102
Antiochus VII, I:87
Antipater, I:104
Antipater (son of Herod), I:105
Antiprotons, IV:153, 154
Anti-Semitism, III:14, 52, 86; IV:22, 48, 80, 109, 154, 176; V:28, 56; VI:127, 166, 186 ; VII:20, 28, 72, 152; VIII:145; X:118
Antoinette Perry (Tony) Award, VI:124
Antokolsky, Mark, III:11 ff
Antonia, citadel, I:105
Antonius, I:104
Antwerp, II:191
Apiru, I:14, 16
Appalachian Spring, VI:46
Aquinas, Thomas, IX:116
Arab League, II:330; VII:138
Arab Legion, II:296, 298, 300, 301, 303
Arab Liberation Army, II:299, 303; VII:14
Arabah I:28; Sea of, 40
Arabia, Arabians, I:14, 37, 50, 57, 74
Arabic II:180-183; VIII:84
Arabs, I:122, 131, 151; II:270-4, 278, 279, 296-300, 301-303, 306, 308, 309, 310, 327
Arad, I:27
Aragon, I:163-165
Arak el Amir, I:83
Aram, Arameans, I:13, 35, 36, 40, 49, 50, 54, 57
Aram-Damascus, I:35, 37, 39, 40
Aram-Zoba, I:35
Ararat, II:245
Arbeiter Ring, II:251
Archelaus, I:105, 106
Archeology, V:80
Argentina, II:219, 237, 281
Ari, see Luria, Rabbi Isaac
Aristobulus I, I:99
Aristobulus II, I:102, 104
Aristobulus (son of Miriam, the Hasmonean), I:105
Arlosoroff, Dr. Haim, VII:90; VIII:15 ff, 178
Armenians VII:28
Armistice Israel-Arab, II:304, 308, 309, 310
Armstrong, Henry, X:140

Arnold, Edward, VI:11 ff
Aron, Herman, V:11 ff, 65
Aronson, Sarah, VII:25 ff
Art, Biblical restriction against, III:44, 62
Artaxerxes I, I:77, 78
Arthritis, IV:142
Art of Boxing, The, X:120
Aryans, II:215, 285, 286, 293
Asa, I:38
Ashdod, I:49, 54; II:324, 326
Asher, tribe, I:27, 29
Ashi, Rab, I:143
Ashkelon (Ascalon), I:29, 84, 99, 136
As I See It, IX:170
Ashkenazim, I:157, 163; II:180, 181, 184, 185, 186, 188, 197, 200; IX:59
Ashteroth Karnaim, I:14
Ashurnasirpal II, I:39
Asluj, II:304
Assefat Nivcharim, VIII:188
Assimilation, Theory of, VIII:36
Assurbanipal, I:57
Assyria, Assyrians, I:13, 35, 39, 40, 49-51, 54, 57-59, 60
Astronomy, V:48 ff
Atlantics of Brooklyn, X:128
Athaliah, I:39, 49
Atlee, Clement, VIII:192
Atom Splitting, V:86-88; structure of, IV:150, 156
Atom bomb, IV:32, 33, 38, 52, 54, 58, 132, 134, 154, 171; V:94
Atomic Conference at the Weizmann Institute in Rehovot, IV:132
Atomic Energy Commission, U.S., IV:140; V:96
Atomic research, II:324, 326; IV:24, 30, 50, 60 ff, 136, 150, 170; V:32, 86, 94, 126
Atomic submarine, V:98, 102
Atomic weapons, IV:138, 140, 170
Atoms for Peace Prize, IV:172
Attell, Abraham, X:15 ff
Auer, Leopold, VI:70
Auerbach, Arnold, X:19 ff
Augsburg, I:155
Auja el Hefir, II:304
Auric, Georges, VI:120
Auschwitz, II:288, 292
Australia, II:281
Australia and New Zealand Army Corps (ANZAC), VII:114
Australian Imperial Forces, VII:114, 116
Australian Military Heroes, VII:114
Australian National Singles, X:152
Austria, Jews in, II:209, 211, 213, 236, 239, 256, 270, 286, 289, 290, 293
Auto-Emancipation: An Appeal To His People By A Russian Jew, IX:126
Automobile, V:76 ff
Automotive engineering, V:76
Auto racing, X:138
Autumn Poems, VI:38
Aviation, V:64, 84, 122
Avineri, Yitzhak, IX:131
Axis, VII:86

B

Baal, VII:68
Baal Shem Suite, VI:40
Baal Shem Tov, Rabbi Israel, II:227, 228, 229; IX:31 ff, 138
Baal Toledoth, II:229
Baasha, I:38
Ba'ath Party, VII:38
Babel, II:73-77 (see also Babylon)
Babylon, I:57, 58, 59, 62-64, 86, 123, 141, 142, 143, 145, 155, 161, 164, 166; II:178; VIII:174, 176
Babylonia, VIII:174, 176
Baccides, VII:102
Bacteriology, V:28, 29
Badran, Shamseddin, III:343
Baeck, Rabbi Leo, IX:21 ff
Baghdad, I:152, 159; II:187
Bagohi, I:91
Balfour, Arthur J., VIII:194, 196
Balfour Declaration, II:239, 256, 265, 271, 276, 278, 279; VIII:96, 168, 194; IX:54, 144
Balkans, I:163; II:180, 208, 213
Bands, VI:60
Bapte, Norval, X:74
Barak ben Abinoam, VII:56
Barak Canyon, II:327
Barany, Robert, IV:15 ff
Barbarian, VI:12
Barcelona, I:162, 163; II:184
Bar Kochba, Simon (Bar Kosiba), I:121, 123, 124, 128; VII:29 ff; IX:176
Barna, Victor, X:23 ff
Barrymore, Ethel, VI:12
Baruch, Bernard M., VIII:19 ff

Bar Yokhai, Simon, II:184
Baseball, X:40, 58, 86, 90, 126
Bashan, I:28, 49
Basketball, X:20, 34, 66, 156, 160; Hall of Fame, 162
Basle, II:233, 234, 272
Batavian National Assembly, II:206
Bath-sheba, VII:46
Bat Yam, I:80
Bayer, Adolf von, IV:162
Beadle, George Wells, IV:96
Becquerel, Antoine Henri, IV:104
Beecham, Sir Thomas, VI:76
Beerot Yitzhak, II:302
Beersheba, II:302, 303
Begin, Menahem, VII:132
Beit-Alpha, I:136; II:266
Beit Arava, II:297
Beit-El, I:28, 29, 37, 50, 86
Beit-Horon, I:40, 97
Beit-Shean, I:27, 29, 31
Beit Shearim, V:82; catacombs, I:127, 129-135
Beit Yosef, (The House of Joseph) IX:58
Beit-Zur, I:86-97; VII:98
IX:58
Belgium, Jews in, II:281
Bell Telephone Co., V:20
Belzec, II:292
Ben-Bezalel, Judah Low, IX:27 ff; II:193
Ben David, Anan, II:178
Ben ei Israel, V:17
Ben-Eliezar, Israel (Baal Shem Tov), II:227-229; IX:31 ff, 138
Ben Gurion, David, II:306, 310; VIII:25 ff, 66, 181, 187; IX:142, 176
Ben Hadad I, I:38
Ben Hadad, III, I:40
Ben Hophni, Shmuel, II:183
Ben Israel, Menasseh, Rabbi, II:190, 195
Benjamin, region, I:34, 37, 63, 64; tribe, 29, 31, 32, 36
Benjamin, Judah P., VIII:33 ff
Benjamin of Tudela, II:187; V:15 ff
Ben Joseph, Akiba, IX:35 ff
Benny Goodman Story, The, VI:63
Benny, Jack, VI:15 ff
Ben Tabeel, I:50
Ben Uri, Bezalel, III:15 ff, 118
Benveniste, Don Avraham, I:163
Ben Yehuda, Eliezer, IX:39 ff
Benz, Karl, V:76
Ben Zakkai, Rabbi Yohanan, I:127; IX:43 ff
Benzoporphyrin, IV:44
Ben Zvi, Itzhak, II:273, 310, 311, 327; VIII:37 ff, 66
Ber, Dov, IX:138
Berbers, VIII:84
Berger, Isaac, X:27 ff
Bergson, Henri, IX:19 ff
Beri-Beri, V:41
Berkshire Music Festival, VI:106
Berlin, II:199, 213, 232, 292
Berlin Academy of Art, III:76, 78
Berlin, Congress of, II:208, 218
Berlin Conservatory, VI:104
Berlin, Irving, VI:21 ff
Berlin Museum for Art Work, III:20
Berlin Symphony Orchestra, VI:114, 165
Berlin University, V:60
Berliner, Emil, V:19 ff
Bernhardt, Sarah, VI:25 ff
Bernstein, Leonard, VI:31 ff
Bessarabia, II:209
Beta disintegration, IV:132
Betar, I:124, 128
Bethlehem, I:35; II:338
Bevatron, IV:152
Bevin, Ernest, VIII:180, 192
Bezalel Art School, III:16, 18, 54, 60, 88, 118, 120, 135
Bezalel Museum & Art Institute, II:326
Bezek, I:28, 29
Bialik, Hayim Nachman, II:219, 278, 280; III:116; IX:47 ff
Bible, IX:54
Biblical military heroes, VII:41 ff, 55 ff, 67 ff, 75 ff, 77 ff, 85 ff, 113 ff, 117 ff, 138
Biblical themes in art, III:46, 62, 87, 98, 120, 160
Biblical Way, The, VI:170
Bieber, Isadore, X:70
Big Betrayal, The, IX:170
Bilu, VIII:178; IX:128
Bir Asluj, II:304
Bir Gafgafa, II:339
Birkenau, II:288, 292
Biro-Bidjan, II:265
Bizet, Georges, VI:66
"Black Day," VII:116
Black Plague, V:44, 45
"Black Saturday," VII:14
Bleichroder, II:213

Bloch, Ernest, VI:37 ff
Bloch, Felix, IV:23 ff
"Block-Floquet Principle," IV:24
"Bloch-Gruneisen Ratios," IV:24
Bloch's Wall, IV:24
Blondell, Joan, VI:41 ff
Blood Libel, I:148, 149; II:203
Blood transfusions, IV:90
Blood types, IV:90
Blue Veil, VI:42
Bluebird of Happiness, The, VI:144
Blum, Leon, II:278, 281; VIII:43 ff
Blum, Walter, X:29 ff
B'nai B'rith, II:252; VIII:106
Board of Deputies of British Jews, II:280
Bohemia, I:165
Bohr, Niels, IV:29 ff, 58, 87, 132
Bolshevik Revolution, VI:100
Bolshoi Opera, VI:142
Bonaparte, Joseph, VII:112
Bontche The Silent, IX:122
Book of Ecclesiastes, IX:176
Book of Legends (or Agadah), The, IX:52 ff
Book of Psalms, III:24; IX:176
Book of Tales, The, IV:14
Bordeaux, II:191, 192, 203, 206
Born, Max, IV:87
Borochov, Dov-Ber, II:239
Boston Braves, X:88
Boston Celtics, X:20, 21, 66, 160
Boston Symphony Orchestra, VI:105
Botany, V:28, 68
Botvinnik, Mikhail, X:136
Boulanger, Nadia, VI:44
Bowles, Chester, VIII:162
Bowling, X:164
Boxing, X:16, 36, 106, 118, 140
Boykoff, Harry, X:33 ff
Brandeis, Louis D., II:248, 276; VIII:47 ff, 109; IX:144
Brazil, II:192, 242, (map), 243
Breslau, II:213
Brice, Fanny, VI:83
Bridal Canopy, The, IV:14
British Army, VII:48, 72 ff, 86 ff, 130
British Conservative Party, VIII:60
British Empire, (see also England, Jews in, II:256, 281
British Government, VIII:58 ff, 156 ff, 190 ff
British Labor Party, VIII:108, 190
British Mandate in Palestine, II:270-76, 278-80, 282, 286, 296, 298, 300, 301, 306, 308; VII:106, 122, 128, 134, 142
British Parliament, VIII:190
British Royal Commission, VIII:100
British Royal Society, IV:92
British "White Paper", VIII:178
Britton, Jack, X:108
Brno, II:217
Brooklyn Atlantics, X:126
Brooklyn Bridge, V:130, 132
Brooklyn Dodgers (football), 54
Brothers Ashkenazi, The, VI:176
Brown Jews, V:17
Brueghel, Peter, II:179
Bubble Chamber, IV:66
Buber, Martin, II:269; VIII:187; IX:53 ff
Budko, Joseph, III:19 ff
Bullfighting, X:48
Bund, II:235, 237, 268
Burke's Law, VI:42
Burma Road, II:302; VII:108
Byzantium, I:134, 136, 152; II:180

C

Cabala, II:184, 201, 226, 228; IV:134; IX:63
Cabalists, IX:114
Ca-eleh Hayu (They Were Like This) III:54
Caesarea, I:104, 141; VII:32
Cagney, James, VI:42
Cahan, Abraham, II:249
Caleb, clan, I:30; VII:80
Calvin, Melvin, IV:35 ff
Cambyses, I:75
Canaan, Canaanites, I:12-14, 15 (map, 16, 26-30, 32, (map) 34; VII:44, 56-58, 68, 80
Canada, Jews, in, II:192, 281
Cancan, VI:134
Cancer, IV:92, 96, 102, 166, 168
Cantion, Shorty, X:138
Cantique de Jerusalem, VI:122
Cantonist system, II:209
Cantor, Georg, V:23 ff
Carbonate of soda, V:90
Carchemish, I:50
Carmen Jones, VI:66
Carnegie Hall, VI:53, 62, 166, 180
Caro, Rabbi Joseph, II:200; IX:57 ff
Carousel, VI:67

Carpentier, Georges, X:108
Caribbean Islands, II:192
Cast a Giant Shadow, VII:108
Castel, II:299
Castile, I:162, 163, 165
Cat and the Fiddle, The, VI:96
Cell creation, process of, IV:118
Central Conference of American Rabbis, II:247
Cervi, Al, X:156
Cezanne, III:112
Chag Ha-Geulah, IX:140
Chagall, Marc, III:25 ff
Chain, Ernst Boris, IV:39 ff
Chaldea, Chaldeans, I:50, 57, 59, 63, 64
Chamber Theatre, II:326
Chamberlain, Neville, II:279; VII:74
Chamberlain, Owen, IV:150
Chants Hebraiques, VI:122
Chassidic Tales, IX:122
Chazars, VIII:174, 176
Chebar, I:64
Chelmno, II:290, 292
Chemical compounds, IV:162
Chemical fertilizers, IV:70
Chemistry, Industrial, IV:163
Chemistry Prize, IV:36, 70, 162, 174
Chemotropism, V:28
Chess, X:44, 94
Chess and Checker Club, Detroit, X:134
Chess Association, Western, X:136
Chess Championship, U.S., X:136
Chicago Bears, X:110
Chicago Cubs, X:86
Chicago White Sox, X:86
Chloroform, IV:72
Chlorophyll, IV:36, 174; V:28
Cholera, V:29
Chopin, VI:132
Chorazin, I:122
Choshen Hamisphat, IX:59
Choynski, Joe, X:35 ff
Christianity, I:107, 109, 128, 132-134, 136, 141, 146-150, 151, 152, 153, 156-158, 162, 163, 166; II:178-182, 184, 185, 186, 190, 191, 193, 196, 206, 208, 209, 214, 216, 220, 232, 233, 244, 252, 254, 327
Christophe Colomb, VI:122
Chromosomes, IV:96
Churchill, Winston, II:271; IV:33; VII:74, 114; VIII:190
Cigar Makers Union, VIII:80
Cincinnati Red Stockings, X:88, 126, 127
Cincinnati, University of, X:90
City College of New York, X:34, 54 66, 168
Civil War, VIII:34
Clarinetist, VI:60
Claudel, Paul, VI:120, 122
Clemenceau, Georges, VII:64; VIII:120
Cleveland (Football) Indians, X:53
Cleveland Institute of Music, VI:38, 40
Cobb, Ty, X:86
Cocteau, Jean, VI:120
Co-enzyme A, IV:100, 102
Cohanim, VII:80
Cohen, Eli, VII:29 ff
Cohn, Hermann, II:269
Cohn, Ferdinand, V:27 ff
Cold War, V:96
Cologne, I:164
Colonne, Edouard, VI:52
Columbia University, II:244; X:48, 110, 112, 170
Comedians, VI:16, 82, 90
Comédie Francaise, VI:26
Comité des Délégations Juives (Committee of Jewish Representatives), VIII:78
Commentary, Rashi's, IX:130 ff
Communism, IV:128
Communist Manifesto, VIII:112
Communist Revolution, II:210, 256, 265
Completely Blue Donkey, The, III:55
Composers, VI: 31, 38, 44, 56, 96, 104, 116, 120, 134, 168, 186
Computers, V:150
Conductors, VI:32, 100, 104, 164
Confederacy, VIII:34, 36
Conference on Claims Against Germany, VIII:78
CIO (Congress of Industrial Organizations), VIII:73, 74
Congress of Soviet Writers, IV:128
Congress, U.S., VIII:104
Congressional Medal for Distinguished Civilian Achievement, V:112
Connecticut, Governor of, VIII:160
Conservative Judaism, II:245, 249
Conservative Party, British, VIII:190
Constantine, I:132
Conventional Lies of Our Civilization, The, VIII:144
Coolidge Prize, VI:38
Copland, Aaron, VI:43 ff, 62, 102
Corbett, Jim, X:36

Cordova, IX:84, 114
Corinth, III:134, 162
Corticosterone, IV:144
Corot, Jean, III:110
Cosmic radiation, IV:150
Cosmic Ray Theory, V:96
Council of Jewish Congregations, VII:72
Counsellor-at-Law, VI:130
Court Jews, II:192, 198
Cousy, Bob, X:20
Cox, Harold, V:106
Cracow, II:214
Cracow Academy of Art, III:52
Cremieux, II:204
Cremieux, Adolphe, VIII:53 ff
Crescas, Rav Hasdai, I:163
Crimea, II:265
Critics Award, VI:68
Crociato, VI:116
Cross of George, VII:134
Crucible, The, VI:127
Crusades, 147, 148, 150, (map) 182, 185, 187, 327
Cry, the Beloved Country, VI:188
Cubist sculpting, III:84
Cultural Exchange, VI:64, 144, 179
Culture Corps, VI:144
Cummings, Wild Bill, X:138
Curtis Institute in Philadelphia, VI:33
Cushan-Rishataim, I:30
Cybernetics, V:150
Cyclotron, IV:152, 153
Cyrenaica, I:107, 108
Cyprus, I:107; II:281, 308
Cyrus, I:74-76
Czechoslovakia, Jews in, II:256, 270, 288, 290, 299

D

Daguerre, Louis, IV:104
Dale, Sir Henry, IV:108, 109
Damascus, I:29, 38-50; II:203; VII:38
Damascus Affair, VIII:54, 112, 128; IX:88
Damrosch, W., VI:56
Dan, tribe, I:31-37; VII:138
Dancing in the Dark, VI:84
Danish Academy of Science, IV:30
Darius, I:75, 76
Dartmouth College, II:244
Davar, VIII:178, 186
Darwin's Theory of Evolution, V:29
David King, I:29, 35, 36, 37 (map), 50; VI:122; VII:41 ff
David and Goliath, VI:108
David royal house, I:40, 57, 59, 62, 75, 76, 142, 159
Davidson, Jo, III:33 ff
David, tower of, I:101
Da Vinci, Leonardo, V:38
Davis, Jefferson, VIII:36
Davis Cup, X:152
Dayan, Moshe, II:301, 334; VII:12, 47 ff 136
Dead of the Wilderness, The, IX:50
Dead Sea, V:82
Dead Sea Scrolls, I:98; IX:172
Death of a Salesman, VI:124, 127
Deborah, I:30; VII:55 ff, 68
Deborah, Song of, VII:58
Degania, II:267, 302; VII:48
Degas, III:112
De Gaulle, Gen. Charles, VIII:125, 126
Delcroze, Jacques, VI:38
Delilah, VII:140
Delinquent Man, The, V:74
Dembitzer, Salamon, II:277
Democracy in Crisis, VIII:108, 110
Dempsey, Jack, X:104
Deoxyribonucleic acid, IV:78
Desert Song, The, VI:66
Detroit Tigers, X:58, 60
Detroit Wolverines, X:54
Diamond Jim Brady, VI:12
Dinah, I:15
Diphtheria, V:118
Direct current, V:139
Displaced Persons, II:308
Disraeli, Benjamin, II:217; VIII:44 ff, 57
DNA, IV:78
Dr. Zhivago, IV:126, 128, 130
Dodecanese Islands, I:107
Dohm, Ch. W., II:196
Dolly Sisters, The, VI:84
Dori, Yaakov, II:300; IX:174
Dostrovsky, Israel, V:31 ff
Dov Ber, Rabbi, of Mezzeritz, II:229
Down in the Valley, VI:187
Dreyfus, Alfred, VI:132; VII:59 ff; VIII:88, 144, 146
Dreyfuss, Barney, X:39 ff
Druzes, II:327
Duke of Wurtemberg, VIII:148
Dwelling Places of Death, IV:146
Dybbuk, The, II:326; VI:162, 176

E

Easy Come, Easy Go, VI:12
Eban, Abba S., II:334; VIII:61 ff
Eben Haezer, I:32
Edison, Thomas Alva, V:14, 22, 140
Edom, Edomites, I:27-29, 35, 36, 37, 39-50, 64, 84, 99, 102, 104, 105
Egypt, Egyptians, I:13-16, 25-27, 29, 30, 35, 36, 37-39, 50, 54, 58, 59, 63, 64, 77, 79, 82, 83, 86-88, 107, 108, 141, 152, 159, 161; II:183, 279, 300, 302-304, 306, 308, 309, 310, 330, 332, 337, 340, 343
Egyptian Army, VII:14, 54
Ehrlich, Paul, IV:43 ff, 92
Ehud, I:30
Eichmann, Adolf, II:287, 288, 311
Ein Gedi, I:123; II:327; V:82
Ein Harod, II:267
Einsatzgroppen, II:290
Einstein, Albert, II:219, 248, 269; III:34; IV:24, 30, 47 ff, 60, 122, 124, 132, 156, 170; V:87, 140; VII:86
Eisenhower, Dwight D., VII:104
Eisenstein, Sergei, VI:47 ff
Ekion, I:98
El-Al, II:324
Elam, Elamites, I:12, 13
El Alamein, VII:12; campaign, 88
Elan Vital, IV:20
El Arish, II:337
El Asifa ("Storm") II:330
Elath, I:37, 49; II:303, 304, 310, 324; Gulf of, II:309, 310
Elazar ben Shmuel, Rabbi, II:195
Eleazar, I:107
Electric conductor, V:52
Electric Meter, V:12, 14
Electromagnetic waves, V:52, 65
Electromagnetism, V:52
Electronics, V:20
Elephantine, I:64, 77, 79
Eli, I:32
Eli, IV:146
Eliahu Golomb, II:255
Eliezer of Worms, Rabbi, II:185
Elijah, I:40
Elijah of Vilna, IX:61 ff
Eliot, T.R., IV:108
Elishib, I:78
Elisha, I:40
El Kontilla, II:338, 339
Elliott, Maxine, VI:12
Elliptic functions, Jacobian, V:56
Elman, Mischa, VI:51 ff
Elman String Quartet, VI:53
El-Paran, I:14
Eltigeh, I:54
El Transito Synagogue, I:164
Emin, I:14
Emmaus, I:97
Energy, IV:82, 100, 118
Engineering, V:130
Engineering, Electrical, V:136
England (see also British Empire); Jews in, I:146, 148, 150, 151, 152, 164; II:180, 190, 192, 194, 202, 204, 208, 212, 219, 256, 270, 280, 281
English-Jewish Society, VII:120
Enzymes, IV:78, 168
Ephraim, I:28-30, 32, 34, 37, 38, 50; tribes, I:29, 31; region VII:44, 78
Epstein, Sir Jacob, III:37 ff
Epstein, Yehuda, III:41 ff
Esarhaddon, I:57
Eshkol, Levi, II:332; VIII:65 ff
Eshkol Publishing Company, VIII:76
Esperantesto, La, IX:178
Esperanto, IX:178 ff
Espionage, VII:36 ff, 60
Essenes, I:109
Esther, I:78
Esterhazy, Major Ferdinand W., VII:60, 66
Ethbaal, I:39
Ethereal Oils, IV:162
Eternal Road, The, VI:187
Eumenides, Les, VI:122
Euphrates, I:12, 50, 64, 77
Europe, Jews in, I:141, 147, 149, 151, 152, 153, 163, 165, 167; II:179, 181, 188, 190-197, 202, 204, 206-215, 216 (map), 216-219, 220, 226-239, 240, 243, 244, 245-248, 256, 268, 276, 279, 281, 282, 284, 290, 293, 308
European Nuclear Center in Geneva, IV:128
Even Ha-Ezer, IX:59
Evil-Merodach, I:74
Exclusion Principle, IV:132
Ex Libris, III:24
Exodus, I:16, 25, 26; modern, II:282
Expressionism, III:137
Ezekiel, I:62, 73
Ezion Geber, I:37
Ezra, I:77, 147; VIII:140

F

Faluja, II:303
Family Carnovsky, The, VI:176
Farm Credit Administration, VIII:134
Fawzi el Kaukji, II:299
Fawzi, Lt. Gen. Mohammed, II:332
Fedayun, II:310
Federal Farm Board, VIII:134
Federal Theater Project, VI:127
Federinko, Nicolai, II:339
Feinberg, Absolom, VII:28
Fencing, X:78
Ferber, Edna, VI:96, 98
Fermi, Enrico, IV:24, 138, 154; V:86-88, 95
Fermi Prize, IV:172
Feynmann, Richard, IV:53 ff
Fiddler on the Roof, IX:16
Finkelstein, Louis, IX:65 ff
First Temple, V:80
First Zionist Congress, VIII:90
Fischer, Albert, IV:101
Fischer, Bobby, X:43 ff
Fischer, Tybor, X:170
Fission, V:88
Fitzsimmons, Bob, X:37
Fitzsimmons, "Sunny Jim", X:122
Five Books of Moses (The Pentateuch), IX:123
Five Pieces for Orchestra, VI:170
Flag is Born, A, VI:132
Flavian kings, I:127
Flavius, Josephus, IX:63
Fleg, Edmond, VI:38
Fleming, Sir Alexander, IV:40
Flora of the Jews, The, V:68
Florey, Sir Howard, IV:40
Florus, I:111
Fly With Me, VI:66
Focus, VI:127
Football, X:52, 56, 82, 110
Forbes Field, X:41
Fordham, X:56
Foreign Affairs Committee, VIII:160
Forest Hills, X:98
Four Lands, Council of, I:165, 168; II:198
France
 army, VII:60; government, VIII:44 ff, 54 ff, 120 ff, 124 ff; Jews in, I:141, 152, 158, 162; II:179, 181, 186, 190, 192, 193, 204, 206, 207, 216, 218, 278, 290; military heroes, VII:110
Franck, James, IV:57 ff
Frank, Jacob, II:226, 227
Frankel, Zecharia, II:227
Frankfurter, Felix, VIII:51, 74, 109
Frankfurt-on-Main, I:150; II:191, 194, 198
Frankists, II:226, 227
Franklin, Benjamin, III:166
Franklin Medal, IV:172
Franklin, Sidney, X:47 ff
Frederick II, I:148, 150
"Free association", V:36
Free French Movement, VIII:125
Free Synagogue, VIII:132
Free Union for Orthodox Jewish Affairs, IX:94
Freiheit (Freedom), VII:94
French Academy of Sciences, IV:104
French National Assembly, II:206
French Revolution, II:193, 196, 206; VII:110
Freud, Sigmund, II:219; V:35 ff
Freudian slip, V:36
Frishman, II:219
Fried, Alfred Herman, IV:61 ff
Friedman, Benny, X:51 ff
Friml, Rudolph, VI:66
Frisch, Otto, V:86-88
From Jewish Life, VI:40
Funk, Casimir, V:39 ff
Funny Girl, VI:184
Futurity, X:122

G

Gabinius, I:102
Gabirol, Shlomo Ibn, IX:71 ff
Gadara, I:84
Gader, I:136
Gadot, II:340
Gaiety Theater; England, VI:28
Galilee, I:29, 30, 34, 38, 50, 54, 58, 64, 86, 99, 105, 107, 111, 130, 133, 141; II:273, 297, 298, 299, 300, 302, 303, 326; Sea of, I:84, 102; II:266, 302
Gallus, I:133
Gallipoli, VII:114
Gamliel, Rabbi (of Yavneh), I:127
Gamliel, Rabbi (ben Yehudah), I:130, 132
Gamliel, Rabbi (VI), I:133
Gamma-globulin, V:108, 110

Gas warfare, IV:174
Gates, Thomas S., V:98
Gaulan (Golan), I:105
Gaza, I:83, 84, 136; II:310, 338
Gaza Strip, II:304, 310, 337
Gedaliah (u) ben Ahikam, I:62, 63, 64
Geiger, Abraham, II:227; IX:94
General Electric, V:136, 140
Genetic control, IV:78
Geneva, II:271
Geonim, I:143, 160, 161, 166; II:178, 179, 183
George, Lloyd, VII:116; VIII:196
Gerlach, Walter, IV:156
German literature, IV:74, 146
Germany
 government, VIII:148, 152 ff
Germany, Jews in, II:186, 187, 190, 192, 194, 197, 199, 202, 204, 206, 209, 214, 216, 217, 219, 232, 233, 256, 269, 270, 283, 284, 285, 288, 290, 294
Gershom, Rabbenu, Meor Hagolah, I:163, 166; II:184, 185
Gershwin, George, VI:22, 55 ff, 66, 68
Gershwin, Ira, VI:58
Gestapo, II:287
Gezer, I:29, 36, 86
Ghirondi, Rav Jonah, I:167
Ghosts, VI:162
Gibeah, I:32
Gibeon, I:29
Gibon, VII:82
Gideon, I:30; VII:67 ff
Gihon spring, I:54
Gilead, I:30, 31, 34, 39, 50; VII:44, 76, 78
Ginzberg, Louis, II:249
Gischala (Gush Halav), I:107
Glaser, Donald Arthur, IV:65 ff
Glicenstein, Henryk, III:45 ff
Glueck, Nelson, IX:75 ff
God and Nature, VI:116
God Bless America, VI:22
God of Vengeance, The, VI:176
Goering, Hermann, II:290
Goethe, IV:74, 128
Golan, I:105
Golan Heights, II:343
Goldberg, Arthur J., VIII:71 ff
Goldberg, Marshall, X:55 ff
Golden Gloves, X:140
Goldmann, Nahum, II:271; VIII:75 ff
Golem of Prague, II:193
Goliath, VII:42
Golomb, Eliyahu, VIII:66
Gompers, Samuel, VIII:79 ff
Gone With the Wind, VI:86
Good Earth, The, VI:132
Goodman, Benny, VI:59 ff
Gordin, Jacob, VI:176
Gordon, Aaron David, II:266; IX:79 ff
Gottlieb (Moshe), Maurycy, III:49 ff
Graf Zeppelin, V:122
Grammar of Politics, VIII:108
Granada, II:181
Grand Duchess of Gerolstein, The, VI:136
Grande Armée, VII:112
Grange, Red, X:52
Great Britain (see British Empire, England)
Great Synagogue, Tel Aviv, II:325
Great Synod, I:99
Greece, Greeks, I:82, 99, 104, 107, 109, 111; II:180
Greek-Syrian Rule of Palestine, VII:98
Greenberg, Hank, X:57 ff, 90
Grey, Sir Edward, VIII:168
Grofé, Ferde, VI:102
Guerrilla warfare, VII:98
Guide To The Perplexed, IX:114
Gulf of Aqaba, II:332, 339
Gun powder, IV:72
Gush Etzion, II:297, 298, 301
Gutmann, Nahum, III:53 ff, 122
Gvulot, II:297

H

Ha-Admor Ha-Zaken, See Shneour Zalman of Lyady, IX:140
Ha'am, Achad, see Achad Ha'am
"Ha-Aretz", IX:14
Habad, II:228; IX:138
Habad Movement, IX:139
Haber, Fritz, IV:69 ff
Habima, II:280, 326; III:116; VI:162, 174
Habiru (Hapiru), I:14, 27
Habsburg, II:192
Hadassah, II:252, 280
Had Gadya (one Kid), III:22
Hadrian, I:123, 125, 127, 128; VII:30
Haffkine, Mordecai, Waldemar, V:43 ff
Haganah, II:273, 275, 296, 300; VII:12, 48, 104, 128, 134, 136; VIII:30, 69; IX:174

Haggadah, III:22; V:138
Haggai, I:76
Hague, The, IV:63
Hahn, Dr. Otto, V:86, 88
Haifa, II:255, 270, 300, 324, 325, 326, 327
Hajos, Alfred, X:61 ff
Ha-Kuzari ("The Chazar"), IX:84
Halacha, I:143; II:200, 226, 249; IX:63
Ha-Levi, Judah, IX:83 ff
Halevi, Ludwig, VI:134
Halevi, Rabbi Yitzhak, IX:130
Halutzim, II:266, 267, 279, 290
Hamath, I:35, 39, 40
Hamburg, II:191, 196, 197, 205, 272
Hamburger, Charles, VI:56
Ha-Meassef, IX:123
Hammath by Gadara, I:136
Hammerstein, Oscar II, VI:65 ff, 98
Hammurabi, I:14
Hanita, II:297
Hannah, I:32
Hanover, II:192
Hans Christian Andersen, VI:92
Hanukkah, VII:98
Ha-Omer, IV:12
Hapoel Hatzair (Young Worker), VIII:16, 66
Har-El (Mountain of God) Brigade, VII:122
Hareubeni, David, II:187
Harosheth of the Gentiles, I:30
Harran, I:50
Hart, Basil Liddell, VII:114, 116
Hartford Nutmegs, X:127
Hartuv, II:298
Hashomer, II:267; VII:154
Ha-Shomer Ha-Tsair, VII:20
Hasidic Themes in Art, III:68
Hasidei Ashekenaz, II:186
Hasidim, IV:14
Hasidim, Hasidism, II:199, 202, 219, 228, 229, 230, 236, 323; IX:56, 62, 63, 64, 138, 140
Haskala, II:199, 202, 206, 216; III:52; IX:63, 118
Hasmoneans, I:85, 97, 99, 102, 104, 105, 109; VII:101
Hazor, I:29, 30, 36; VII:56, 58
Health, Education and Welfare, Secretary of, VIII:160
Heavy hydrogen, V:32
Heavy water, V:32
Hebrew Literature, IV:12
Hebrew Union College, II:247, 252, 253
Hebrew University, II:271, 280, 324, 325, 326; V:80, 182; IX:54, 56, 172, 174, 176
Hebron, I:30, 35, 53
Hecht, Ben, VI:132
He-Halutz (The Pioneer), VII:94, 134, 154; VIII:38, 68, 184
Heifetz, Jascha, VI:69 ff
Heine, Heinrich, II:214
Heisenberg, Werner, IV:24
Helen of Troy, VI:136
Helen of Troy, N. Y., VI:83
Heliotropism, V:28
Helium, IV:88
Hellenes, Hellenism, I:76, 79, 82, 83, 99, 104, 105, 107, 109, 133; VII:98
Helvetia Symphony, VI:40
Hemingway, Ernest, X:50
Henry III (of England), I:150
Henry VII (Emperor), I:145
Hep-Hep, II:207
Heredity, IV:96
Herod I, 103 (map), I:104, 105, 107
Herod II (Antipas), I:105
Herschel, Sir William, V:47 ff
Hertz, Dr. Gustav, IV:58
Hertz, Heinrich Rudolf, V:51 ff, 65
Herzl, Dr., VI:176
Herzl, Theodor, II:231, 235, 237, 239; III:42; V:146; VII:66; VIII:76, 87 ff, 96; IX:12, 13, 14, 90, 128, 136
Hess, Moses, IX:87 ff
Heydrich, II:288, 290
Heyse, Paul, IV:73 ff
Hezekiah, I:50, 54, 57
High-priesthood, I:85, 102, 106, 107, 125
Hillel II, I:132
Hillel, School of, I:107, 123, 127
Hiram, I:35, 37
Hirsch, Baron, II:213, 219, 237
Hirsch, Samson Raphael, Rabbi, II:218, 227; IX:91 ff
Hirszenberg, Samuel, III:57 ff, 122
Histadrut, II:280; VIII:40, 66, 69, 178, 186
Historical Judaism, II:245, 249
Hitler, Adolf, II:268, 269, 270, 279, 284; VII:92
Hitties, I:27, 29, 35, 36
Hod, Brigadier Mordechai, II:337
Hodesblatt, Max, X:34
Holbein Studio, III:36
Holland, Bill, X:138

Holland, Jews in, I:154; II:180, 192, 207, 230
Holland, Lou, X:138
Holman, Nat, X:65 ff, 160
Holmes, Oliver Wendell, VIII:51
Holy Cross, X:112
Holy History of Mankind, The, IX:88
Holy Tabernacle, VII:44
Honegger, Arthur, VI:105, 120
Hopkins, Sir Frederick Goland, IV:80
Hore-Belisha, Lord Leslie, VII:71 ff
Horev, campaign, II:304
Horites, I:12
Hormones, IV:102, 142
Horowitz, Vladimir, VI:73 ff
Horse racing, X:30, 70, 122
Hosea, prophet, I:51
Hoshea, king, I:50
Houdin, Jean Robert, VI:80
Houdini, Harry, VI:77 ff
House of Representatives, VIII:162
House Un-American Activities Committee, VI:128
Hovevei Zion (Lovers of Zion), II:229, 238; III:120; VIII:76, 170, 171; IX:128, 136
Hudson River Suite, VI:102
Huguenots, The, VI:118
Huleh valley, II:303
Hull House, VI:60
Humoresque, VI:180
Humphries, Richard, X:118, 119, 120
Hungary, Jews in, II:208, 211, 218, 236, 256, 267
Hurok, Sol, VI:166
Hussein, King, II:332, 334
Husseini, Abdul Monem, II:338
Husseini, Abdel Kadr, II:298
Hydrogen, V:32
Hydrogen bomb, IV:136, 138; V:96, 146
Hymne de Sion, VI:122
Hyrcanus, John I (Jonathan), I:99, 102, 104
Hyrcanus, John II, I:87, 102, 104
Hysko, I:15
Hysteresis Loss, Law of, V:136

I

I and Thou, IX:54
Iberian Peninsula, VIII:174
Ibn David, Abraham (*see* Rabad)
Ibn Ezra, Moses VIII:86
Ibn Ezra, Yehuda, II:182
Ibn Ghazali, II:182
Ibn Tibbon, Yehuda, II:181
Ibsen, Henrik, VI:162
Ibzan of Bethlehem, VII:78
I Can Get It For You Wholesale, VI:182
Ice-Skating, X:74, 144
Ice Skating, International Championships at St. Petersburg, X:144
Idol worship, III:12
Immigration to Israel, *see* Aliyah
Immunization, IV:44, 112
Imperial Chemical Industries, V:92
Imperial Music School, VI:52
Impressionism, III:76, 106, 112, 160, 164
Incident at Vichy, VI:127
Independence, Israel, Declaration of, II:300, 304, 305, 306, 308, 311, 321, 327
India, II:191; VIII:60, 158
Indianapolis, Memorial Day 500, X:138
Indian Love Call, VI:68
Indo-China, VIII:126
Infantile paralysis, V:104, 106, 108, 112
Innocent III, I:147
Inquisition, I:150
Insecticides, IV:72
Institute for Advanced Study in Princeton, IV:30
Institute For Research on Jewish Communities in the Middle East, VIII:42
Institute of Theological Physics in Copenhagen, IV:30
International Research Center for Chemical Microbiology, IV:42
International Thousand Islands Bridge, V:132
In the Beginning, VI:46
Introduction to Politics, An, VIII:110
Iraq, I:152; II:300, 302, 332, 334, 337
Iraq Sweidan, II:303
Irgun, VIII:30, 110
Irgun Zevai Leumi, II:275, 280; VII:130, 142; VIII:30, 110
Isaac, see also Yitzhak
Isaac, I:15
Isaac, Rufus (Lord Reading), II:280
Isaiah, I:51, 54, 75
Ishbaal, VII:44
Ishmael ben Nathaniah, I:63
Ishmaelites, VII:68

Ishtar Gate, I:63
Islam, I:74, 82, 146-148, 151, 152, 156-161, 166; II:178-182, 187, 190, 201, 327
Ismay, General Lord, VII:118
Isotopic carbon, IV:38
Israel Bonds Organization, VIII:132
Israel, Defense Forces, II:331, 334, 337, 338, 339, 343; VII:12 ff, 14, 48 ff, 54, 104
Israel government, II:306, 307; VIII:38 ff, 62 ff, 66 ff, 178 ff, 184, 194
Israeli heroes, VII:11 ff, 122 ff, 129 ff, 134 ff, 147 ff
Israel, Independence Day, II:267; III:26
Israel Kingdom of, I:34-36, 37-40, 49-51, 54-, 60
Israel, Six Day War, *see* Six Day War
Israel, War of Independence, VIII:30; IX:176
Israel, Miracle in the Desert, VII:34
Israel Museum, III:40
Israel Prize, V:84; VI:162
Israels, Joseph, III:61 ff
Issachar, tribe, I:29, 38
Isserlis, Rabbi Moshe, II:200
Italy, Jews in, I:107, 152, 163, 165; II:180, 181, 190, 206, 230, 293
I Was a Fugitive from a Chain-Gang, VI:130

J

Jabotinsky, Ze'ev, II:275; VII:152; VII:95 ff
Jackson, John, X:120
Jacob, I:12, 15, 27
Jacob Joseph, Rabbi (Baal Toledoth), II:229
Jacobi, Karl Gustav, V:55 ff
Jacobian Elliptic Functions, V:56, 57
Jacob's Ladder, VI:170
Jacobs, Hirsch, X:30, 69 ff
Jael, VII:58
Jaffa, I:98, 102, 107; II:297, 298, 299
Jaffee, Irving, X:73 ff
Jaroslav, II:165
Jason, I:86, 88
Javits, Jacob, VIII:101 ff
Jazar, I:27
Jazz, VI:44, 58, 60, 62, 64
Jazz Singer, The, VI:83, 86
Jebusites, I:35
Jeffries, Jim, X:38
Jehoahaz of Israel, I:40
Jehoahaz of Judah, I:50
Jehoash, I:40
Jehoiachin (Konyahu), I:50, 57, 59, 64, 73-75, 142
Jehoiada, I:49
Jehoiakim, I:50, 64
Jehoram, I:40, 49
Jehoshaphat, I:38, 49
Jehu, I:39, 40, 49
Jenin, II:338
Jephthah the Gileadite, I:31; VII:75 ff
Jeremiah, I:59, 62, 63, 64
Jericho, I:27, 28, 29, 104, 106, 136; II:339; VII:80
Jeroboam I, I:37, 38, 50
Jeroboam II, I:40, 49, 51
Jerusalem, I:28, 34, 35, 36, 37, 49-51, 54, 57, 59, 62, 63, 75, 77, 84-86, 88, 97, 101, 102, 104, 105-107, 109, 111, 122, 125, 126, 128, 131, 141; II:178, 179, 187, 279, 280, 296-300, 301, 311, 322, 325-327, 338, 339; VII:44; Battles for, VII:30, 44, 98, 104, 122; Reunification of, II:338, 344; V:80; VII:54, 122 ff; VIII:66, 68
Jerusalem Diary, VIII:18
Jerusalem Post, The, VIII:184
Jessel, George, VI:81 ff
Jesus of Nazareth, I:109, 148
Jethro, I:26
Jewish Agency, II:275, 276, 278, 279; VII:14, 30, 90, 96; VIII:16, 17, 62, 70, 76, 78, 178, 179, 200; IX:142
Jewish Brigade, II:279, 297; VII:88, 136; VIII:80
Jewish Camari Theater, III:32
Jewish Colonization Association, II:307
Jewish Institute of Religion, IX:169
Jewish King Lear, The, VI:176
Jewish Labor Committee, II:251
Jewish Legion, III:40; VII:154; VIII:66
Jewish National Council, IX:54
Jewish National Fund, II:272, 278; III:122; VIII:171
Jewish Publication Society, II:249
Jewish Socialist Association, II:234
Jewish State, The, VIII:88, 144
Jewish Theological Seminary, II:249, 252, 253
Jewish Themes in Art, III:20, 24, 26, 43, 48, 50, 58, 62, 68, 98, 128, 148
Jewish Underground Army, *see* Haganah
Jewish War Veterans, VIII:106
Jews' Oath, VIII:54
Jezebel, I:39, 40
Jezreel Valley, I:27, 30; II:297, 300, 326
Jezreel, VII:56, 68
Joab, VII:46
Joachim, Joseph, VI:165
Joash, I:49
Johanan, High Priest, I:79
John (Jonathan) Hyrcanus I, I:99, 102, 104
John Hyrcanus II, I:87, 102, 104
John Loves Mary, VI:67
Johnson, Jack, X:37
Johnson, Lyndon B., VIII:187
Jolson, Al, VI:85 ff
Jonathan, VII:44
Jonathan Maccabeus, I:98
Joram, I:38
Jordan, Hashemite Kingdom of, II:304, 309, 330, 331, 332, 334, 337, 338, 339, 346
Jordan, River, I:27, 28, 29, 83, 107; II:323; VII:38
Jordan, Valley, II:302
Josef of Pumbeditha, Rabbi, I:143
Joseph and His Brethren, VI:83
Joseph, Tribes, I:28, 29, 30, 32, 35
Joseph II, of Austria, II:195
Josephus, II:201, 217
Joshua, I:27, 29; VII:56, 85 ff
Joshua ben Jozadak, I:75, 76
Joshua, Book of, VII:80, 82
Josiah, I:50, 57
Jotham, I:49
Juarez, VI:132
Judah (*see also* Yehuda), kingdom, I:35, 36, 37-40, 49-51, 54, 57, 59, 62; VII:44, 56; region (*see also* Judea), I:28, 30, 34, 35, 37, 63, 64, 73-79; tribe, I:15, 28, 29, 31, 32
Judah Maccabeus, I:97, 98; VII:97 ff
Judea, I:61, 74, 84-86, 88, 97-99, 100, 102, 104, 105-107, 126, 128, 130; II:326; VII:32; VIII:140
Judges, Book of, VII:56, 58, 68, 70, 76
Jud Suss, *see* Oppenheimer, Joseph
Jugend (Youth), III:80
Julian, I:133
Julius Caesar, I:102, 104
June Is Bustin' Out All Over, VI:68
Jungian Psychology, IV:132
Jupiter, I:127
Justinius, I:136

K

Kabos, Endre, X:77 ff
Kadesh, I:29
Kadesh Barnea, I:15, 26, 27, 28, 49
Kaiser Wilhelm, IV:70
Kaiser Wilhelm Institute, IV:60, 80, 101, 120, 166, 174, 176
Kalischer, Rabbi Zvi, II:229
Kaminski, Daniel David, VI:90
Kansas City Blues, X:88
Karaites, II:178, 179
Karpati, Karely, X:170
Kattowitz, II:229
Katz, Mane, III:67 ff
Katznelson, Berl, VIII:186
Kaye, Danny, VI:89 ff
Kelard, Abraham, X:170
Keller, Helen, III:34
Kendall, Edward Calvin, IV:142, 144
Kenites VII:58
Kennedy, John F., VIII:74, 160
Keren Hayesod, II:276
Keren Kayemet (Jewish National Fund), VIII:170
Kern, Jerome, VI:66, 95 ff, 102
Kessler, David, VI:176
Kfar Blum, VIII:46
Kfar Darom, II:302
Kibbutz, II:266, 267, 279, 323
Kibbutz Deganya, IX:82
Kibbutz Deganya-Bet, VIII:66
Kibbutz Sde Boker, VIII:31
Kibbutz Yad Mordechai, VII:24
Kid from Brooklyn, The, VI:92
Kidron Valley, I:81
Kiev Conservatory, VI:74
King and I, The, VI:67
King Artaxerxes I, VIII:140
King David Hotel, II:280
King Khabbus, VIII:84, 85
King, Mackenzie, V:132
King, Philip, X:81 ff
Kisch, Frederick, VII:85 ff
Kish, Colonel, II:274
Kishenev Pogrom, II:238
Kitah-As-Sirav, IX:114
Kling, John, X:85 ff

Knesset, II:306, 311, 325; VII:14; VIII:63, 70, 94, 181
Koch, Robert, V:29
Kol Nidre, VI:170
Kommer, Edward, V:60
Konice, II:201
Kook, Abraham Isaac Hacohen, II:278; IX:95 ff
Kornberg, Arthur, IV:77 ff
Kosciusko, Thaddeus, VII:160, 162
Kostelanetz, Andre, VI:99 ff
Kots, Vladimir, X:116
Koufax, Sandy, X:89 ff
Koussevitsky, Serge, IV:44, 46, 103 ff
Kraenzlein, Alvin, X:130
Krebs, Sir Hans, IV:79 ff, 100
Kronecker, Leopold, V:26, 59 ff
Kupat Holim, II:280
Kuwait, II:332, 334, 337
Kuzari, II:182

L

Labor Zionist Movement, Germany, VIII:184
Labor Zionist Organization of America, II:251
Lachish, I:54, 55, 56, 59
Lady in the Dark, VI:91
Lady of the Camelias, VI:30
La Fontaine, Jean de, VI:26
Lagerlof, Selma, IV:146
Laish (Leshem), I:31
Landau, Leib Davidovitch, IV:85 ff
Landsteiner, Karl, IV:89 ff
Lasker, Emanuel, X:93 ff
Lasken Prize, IV:82
Laski, Harold J., VIII:107 ff, 178
Lassalle, Ferdinand, VIII:111 ff
Last Time I Saw Paris, The, VI:68, 96
Lateran Council, I:147, 149
Latrun: Prison, VII:14; Road, II:301, 303, 338
Latvia, II:256, 268
Laughter and Creative Evolution, IV:20
League of Nations, II:236, 265, 271, 273; VIII:78, 132, 166
Leah, Tribes I:29
Lebanon, I:36; II:300, 302, 303, 304, 309
Lederberg, Joshua, IV:95 ff
Leeser, Isaac, II:249
Leghorn, II:191
Legion of Honor, VII:66
Lehi (Israel Freedom Fighters), VII:36, 142
Lehman, Herbert, VIII:115 ff
Lemech, II:185
Lend Lease Act, VIII:134
Lenglen, Suzanne, X:97 ff
Lenin Prize, IV:86
Leon (Spain), I:167
Leonard, Benny, X:101 ff, 106
Leopold I, II:191
Lesser, Ury, III:159 ff
Lessing, G. E., IX:118
Let's Face It, VI:91
Levites, I:15, 29, 37, 49, 106
Levy, Asher, II:244
Lewis, Ted "Kid", X:105 ff
Lewisohn Stadium, V:54
Liberal Party, British, VII:72; VIII:190
Liberman, Aaron Samuel, II:234
Liberty in the Modern State, VIII:110
Libya, II:337
Lieben, Robert Von, V:63 ff
Liebermann, Max, III:62, 73 ff, 134, 162
Life on the Mississippi, VI:96
Light, Speed of, IV:122 ff
Lightning, V:136
Likute Amarim (A Collection of Sayings), IX:139
Lilien, Ephraim Moshe, II:230, 269, 277; III:77 ff, 120
Lincoln Portrait, A, VI:102
Linguo Internacia de la Doktoro Esperanto, IX:178
Lipchitz, Jacques, III:81 ff
Lipmann, Fritz, IV:80, 99 ff
Lippman, Gabriel, IV:103 ff
Lipschitz, Yevni, IV:88
Lister Institute, V:40, 104
Lister, Lord, V:45
Literature Prize, IV:12, 22, 74 ff, 126, 146
Lithuania, Jews in, I:151, 152, 153, 154, 163, 164, 165, 167, 168; II:181, 190, 209, 219, 256, 268, 291
Little, George, X:52
Litvinovsky, Pinchas, III:122
Livingstone, Mary, VI:18
Lodge, John, VIII:163
Loew, Emmanuel, V:67 ff
Loewi, Otto, IV:107 ff
Lohamei Herut Yisrael, *see* Lehi
Lombroso, Cesare, V:71 ff
London, II:191, 194, 213, 234

Lord Baltimores, X:127
Los Alamos, IV:26, 54, 154
Los Angeles Dodgers, X:90
Loubet, Emile, VII:66
Louisville Colonels, X:40
Louvre, III:132
Lover, Come Back to Me, VI:68
Lower Depths, The, VI:176
Lubetkin, Tsivia, VII:91 ff
Lublin, I:165; II:228
Luckman, Sidney, X:109 ff
Lunel, II:181
Luria, Rabbi Isaac, II:201, 229; IX:99 ff
Luzzatto, Sinho, II:195
Lwow, II:194
Lydda, I:86, 133; II:296, 303, 324

M

Macbeth, VI:38
Maccabee, Judah, VII:97 ff
Maccabees, I:97, 99
Maccabiah Games, X:170
MacDonald, Ramsay, VIII:192
Macedonia, I:82, 83, 84
Mackinac Straits Bridge, V:130
Madagascar, II:290
Mafraq, II:337
McLarnin, Jimmy, X:140
Magi, I:142
Magician Among the Spirits, A, VI:80
Magicians, VI:78
Magnes, Judah L., II:348; IX:103 ff
Magnetic moments, IV:136, 156
Maharal, *see* Ben Bezalel, Judah Low
Mahoza, I:141
Maimon, Rabbi Yehuda, Leib Hacohen, II:323
Maimon, Allen, X:113 ff
Maimonides (Rambam), I:146, 152, 159, 161; II:181-184, 200, 243, IX:113 ff, 118
Maimonides College, II:249
Mainz, I:164; II:185
Majorca, I:160
Malkieh, II:302
Manara, II:303
Manasseh, King, I:57, 58
Manasseh, tribe, I:29
Mandel, Georges, VIII:119 ff, 125
Manhattan Project, IV:38, 170; V:126
Man who Had all the Luck, The, VI:127
Man Who Never Was, The, VII:118
Mapai (Labor Party of Israel), VIII:40, 41, 63, 178, 188
Marathon, X:148, 150
Marceau, Marcel, VI:107 ff
Marconi, V:52, 65, 140; Company, 114
Marcus, David, II:300; VII:14, 103 ff
Marcus, Siegfried, V:75 ff
Marduk, I:74
Mari, I:12, 14, 16
Maria Theresa, II:203
Marine Workers' Union, VIII:190
Marissa, I:84
Marranas, II:191; VIII:12, 136, 137
Marshall, Lewis, II:249, 278
Marsik, VI:38
Marx, Karl, II:219; IX:88
Masada, VII:30; IX:176
Maskilim (*see* Haskalah)
Massachusetts Institute of Technology, V:150
Massena, Andrea, VII:109 ff
Massoth Rabbi Binyamin (Travels of Rabbi Benjamin), V:16
Mathematics, V:24, 56, 60
Mathewson, Christy, X:92
Matiko, Jan, III:52
Matisse, III:104, 134
Mattaniah (Zedekiah), I:59
Mattathias Antigonus, I:87
Mattathias, HaCohen, VII:98
Maxwell, James Clark, IV:122; V:52
Mazar, Benjamin, V:79 ff
Medal of Merit of the National Academy of Sciences, IV:172
Medes, I:14, 58
Medicine, Nobel Prize, IV:44, 78, 90, 96, 100, 112, 118, 142, 160, 166
Megabysos, I:78
Megiddo, I:30, 36, 37, 58
Meir ben Baruch of Rothenburg, I:162, 163, 164
Meitner, Lise, V:85 ff
Menahem, King, I:51
Menasseh, Ben Israel, II:190, 195
Mendel, Rabbi Menahem, IX:138
Mendele Mocher S'farim, II:219
Mendelssohn, Moses, II:202, 226, 232, 245; IX:117 ff
Mendes-France, Pierre, VIII:123 ff
Mendoza, Daniel, X:106, 117 ff
Menelaus, I:87, 88
Menuhin, Yehudi, VI:111 ff
Meor Hagolah (**see** Gershom, Rabbenu)
Mephiboshet, I:36

Merrick, David, VI:182
Mernephtah, I:29
Mesha, I:38
Mesopotamia, I:12, 14, 15, (map), 27, 36, 50, 64, 152, 158
Messiah, I:36, 136, 141; II:187, 201, 226
Metabolism, IV:102, 168
Metchnikoff, Elie, IV:46, 111 ff
Metropolitan Museum of N.Y., III:166
Metropolitan Opera, VI:142
Meunites I:49
Mexico, II:281
Meyer, Julius, II:245
Meyerbeer, Giacomo, VI:115 ff
Meyerhof, Dr. Otto, IV:101, 117 ff
Mezzeritz, Rabbi Dov Ber of, II:229
Micah, I:51
Michel, M. George, III:128
Michelson, Albert Abraham, IV:121 ff
Michigan, University of, X:52
Michigan Wolverines, X:52
Microphone, V:21
Middle East Center for Arabic Studies, VIII:62
Midian, Midianites, I:16, 26, 30; VII:68
Midrashim, IX:132
Migdal, II:266
Migdal David, III:116
Mikan, George, X:156
Mikve, Israel, VIII:130
Milhaud, Darius, VI:119 ff
Miller, Arthur, VI:123 ff
Miller, Walter, X:121 ff
Milta Pass, II:339
Mi-Maamakim (De Profundis), VI:170
Minhag America, II:247
Miriam the Hasmonean, I:105
Misfits, The, VI:127
Mishmar Haemek, II:299
Mishmar Hayarden, 302
Mishnah, I:124, 125, 130, 131, 132, 143; II:178
Mishnah Torah, II:183; IX:114
Mittnagdim, II:229; IX:62, 64, 140
Mitrani, Rabbi Joseph, VIII:137
Mitropolous, Dmitri, VI:33
Mitzpeh Ramon, II:327
Mizpeh, I:62, 63
Mizrachi, IX:136; Movement, 134
Moab, Moabites, I:27-30, 35, 36, 38, 40
Modigliani, Amadeo, III:87 ff
Mogen David, VII:18
Mohieddin, Zakaria, II:343
Molcho, Shlomo, II:187
Monash, Sir John, VII:113 ff
Mond, Ludwig, V:89 ff
Monet, III:112
Monkey on My Back, X:142
Montagu, Ewen, VII:117 ff
Montefiore, Moses, II:204, 228; VIII:54, 127 ff
Montgomery, General, VII:86, 90
Mood Music, VI:100
Moors, VIII:84
Moravia, I:165; II:201
Morgan, J. Pierpont, VIII:20
Morgenthau, Henry, Jr., VIII:131 ff
Morgenthau, Henry, Sr., VIII:132
Morley, Edwards, IV:124
Morocco, II:334
Morrison, Eli, X:170
Moscow Conservatory, VI:138
Moses, I:16, 27; III:16, 160; VII:80; IX:50, 107 ff
Moses and Aaron, VI:172
Moshav, II:267, 279, 323
Mosley, Oswald, II:280
Motzkin, II:238
Mount Gerizim, I:79
Mount Gilboa, I:35; II:266
Mount Hermon, II:343
Mount Seir, I:14
Mount Scopus, II:330
Mount Sinai, II:309; VII:80
Mount Sinai Hospital, II:244, 253
Mount Zion, VII:46
Moyn, Lord, VII:36
Muni, Paul, VI:129 ff
Munk, II:204
Muscular energy, IV:82, 100, 118
Museum of Modern Art, III:124
Music, VI:Atonal, 170; "Jewish," 38, 40, 46, 120, 122, 144, 170, 172; Modern, 168; Popular, 22, 56, 60, 66, 96, 100, 156, 182
Music Festival in Israel, VI:180
Muslims, IX:84
Myers, Lou, X:138

N

Nabateans, I:84
Nablus, II:339
Nabonides, I:74
Nabopalassar, I:57, 58
Nabu-Naid, I:25
Nachmanides (Rabbi Moshe ben Nachman), II:184
Nachshon, II:299
Nagid, IX:116
Nagrella, Rab Shmuel, I:161
Nahalal, II:267; VII:48
Naphtali, tribe of, I:29; VI:56
Napoleon, II:207; VII:162
Napoleon III, Emperor, VIII:54, 55, 112
Napoleonic Wars, VII:110
Nasser, Gamal Abdel, II:343; VII:7
Nassi, Don David Joseph, VIII:135 ff
Nataniah, II:296
Nathan, VII:44, 46
Nathan the Wise, IX:118
National and University Library, II:324
National Aeronautics and Space Administration, IV:38
National Basketball League, X:156
National Council on the Arts, VI:180
National Defense Research Council, IV:38
National Foundation for Infantile Paralysis, V:106
National Indoor Tennis Championship, X:152
National League, X:40, 86, 90, 92, 127
"Natural selection", IV:20
Nature, IV:82
Nautilus, The, V:98
Navy, X:53
Nazareth, II:299, 302, 326
Nazirites, VII:138
Nazism, II:237, 268, 269, 271, 281, 284, 285, 288, 290, 294; III:36, 86, 157; IV:22, 30, 32, 40, 52, 58, 70, 80, 109, 146, 154, 156, 170, 176; V:76, 86, 92, 94; VI:108, 186; VII:12, 20, 72, 128; VIII:17, 78, 121, 124, 152; IX:142, 170
NCCA, X:168
Nebuchadnezzar, I:50, 59, 63, 64, 73, 74
"Nebulae", V:50
Negev, I:15, 49, 77; II:297, 298, 300, 326, 327, 338
Nehemiah, I:78, 79, 153; VIII:139 ff
Neosalvarsan, IV:46
Nervous System, IV:108; V:142
Netherlands, see Holland
Neutrons, V:86
New Amsterdam, II:203, 235, 242
Newcomb, Simon, IV:122
New Deal, VIII:24, 118
New Foundations for the Theory of Elliptical Functions, V:56
New Light Over Zion, A, IX:134
New Wave, III:134
New York, II:203, 244, 246, 253, 281, 306
New York Art Students League, III:168
New York Critics Circle Award, VI:127
New York Drama Critics Award, VI:124
New York Giants (baseball), X:74, 86
New York Giants (football), X:54, 53
New York, Mutuals of, X:126
New York Philharmonic Orchestra, VI:34, 179
New York University, X:156
New York Whirlwinds, X:66, 160
New York Yankees, X:40, 188
New Zealand, II:281
Nicholas 1, Czar, VIII:128
Nickel, V:90-91
Niepse, Joseph, IV:104
"Night Raiders," VII:48
Nile, I:64, 108
Nili, VII:28
Nineteen Letters on the Jews and Judaism, IX:94
Nightmare Alley, VI:84
No Man Stands Alone, X:142
Noah, Mordecai Manuel, II:245
Nobel, Alfred, IV:62
Nordau, Max, II:232; VIII:143 ff, 172; IX:144
North Africa, I:148, 152; II:180, 183, 190, 192, 218
NATO, IV:140
Northwestern University, X:52
Nostalgia and Nightmare in the Fiction of S. Y. Agnon, IV:12
Notre Dame, X:54, 56, 112
Nubia, I:54, 108
Nuclear Energy, IV:24
"Nuclear induction," IV:28
Numbers, Theory of, V:60
Nuremberg, I:149; II:219; Laws, II:269, 270, 285, 286, 292
Nutrition, IV:82

O

Oak Ridge, IV:32
Oborin, Lev, VI:138
Ochua, Dr. Severo, IV:78
O'Connor, Patrick, X:130

Octavian, I:104
Oedipus Complex, V:38
Offenbach, Jacques, II:227; VI:133 ff
Ohaliab, III:16
Ohel, II:280; III:116
Ohio State, X:53
Ohm, V:12
Oh, What a Beautiful Morning, VI:68
Oistrakh, David, VI:137 ff
Oistrakh, Igor, VI:138, 140
Oklahoma, VI:67
Ol' Man River, VI:68, 98
Olympic Games, X:12, 62, 76, 78; Antwerp, 12; Berlin, 78; Helsinki, 110, 115, 170; London, 114, 168; Melbourne, 28; Paris, 28, 130; Tokyo, 28
Omri, I:38-39
Only Make Believe, VI:68
Opera, VI:116, 142, 186; comic, 134
Operation Meatball, VII:118
Operetta, VI:134
Ophel ostracon, I:51
Ophir, I:37, 40
Oppenheim, Moritz, III:95 ff
Oppenheimer, Joseph, II:192, 195; VIII:147 ff
Oppenheimer, Robert, IV:26, 136, 139; V:93 ff, 146
Organization of Jewish Fighters, VII:92
Or Ganuz (Hidden Light), IX:56
Orach Chaim, IX:59
Oratorio, VI:116
Order of Battle, VIII:106
Orestes Trilogy, VI:122
Oriental Jewish communities, VIII:42
Orion, V:48
Orloff, Chana, III:101 ff
Orpheus in the Underworld, VI:136
Orthodox Judaism, II:218, 245, 248, 249; IX:92, 94
Othniel ben Kenaz, I:30
Ottoman Empire, I:157; II:190, 192, 236
Our New Music, VI:45

P

Pacifism, IV:52, 62 ff
Padan-Aram, I:12
Pale of Settlement, II:196, 210, 256
Palestine, A Bi-National State, IX:56
Palestine Electric Company, VIII:158
Palestine, History of, V:82
Palestine Symphony Orchestra, 280
Palestinian Government, VIII:166
Palestinian Herves, VII:12 ff, 127 ff, 142, 148, 152
Palestinian Liberation Organization, II:332, 337
Palmach, II:296, 300; VII:12 ff, 52, 122, 136; VIII:30
Palmyra, I:37
Pan-America, A Handbook for the Peace Movement, IV:63
Pan-American movement, IV:62
Panion, I:83
Pann, Abel, III:122
Pantomime, VI:108
Pantothenic acid, IV:102
Paran, I:14
Paray, Paul, VI:112
Paris, II:213, 270
Paris Opera House, VI:116
Parliament, VII:72
Parthia, Parthians, I:104, 107, 111, 128, 141, 142
Pashkov, Vassili, IV:88
Pasquino the Mocher, V:68
Pasternak, Boris, IV:125 ff
Pasteur Institute, IV:122
Pasteur, Louis, V:44, 132
Patketikar school of expressionism, III:137
Path of Carbon in Photosynthesis, The, IV:38
Patriarchate, I:122, 123, 127, 130, 132, 133, 134, 156
Paul, I:109
Pauli Exclusion Principle, IV:132
Pauli, Wolfgang, IV:87, 131 ff
Peace Corps, VI:144
Peace Prize, German Book Publishers, IV:146
Peel, Commission, II:278
Peerce, Jan, VI:141 ff
Pekah, I:50
Pellagra, V:41, 42, 72
Penicillin, IV:40, 158
Penny Arcade, IV:42
People Will Say We're in Love, VI:68
Perea, I:106
Pereire, II:213
Peretz, Isaac Leib, II:219; IX:121 ff
Persia, Persians, I:64, 79, 80, 82, 84, 86, 133, 136, 141, 142
Persian Empire, VIII:140, 141

Pescennius Niger, I:130
Petach Tikva, VIII:66
Petahya of Regensburg, II:187
Petain, Henri, VIII:122
Petrograd, State Symphony Orchestra of, VI:105
Phaedon, IX:118
Phagocytes, IV:112
Pharisees, I:99, 106, 107, 109
Phasael, tower, I:101
Philadelphia Athletics, X:88, 126
Philharmonic Orchestra of Berlin, VI:114
Philharmonic School, Moscow, VI:104
Philippus, I:105
Philistia, Philistines, I:30, 32, 34, 36, 40, 50, 54, 58, 64; VII:42, 82 138 ff
Philo, I:108
Phoenicia, I:35, 36, 39, 50, 59, 84, 100
Phonograph, V:22
Photography, Color, IV:104
Photosynthesis, IV:36, 60, 168
Physics Institute in Moscow, IV:88
Physics Prize, IV:24, 30 ff, 48, 54, 58, 66 ff, 80, 86, 104, 122, 132, 136, 150, 156, 170
Physiology & Medicine, Prize, IV:44, 78, 90, 96, 100, 112, 118, 142, 160, 166
Pianists, VI:74, 164
Picasso, III:68
Picquart, Georges, VII:60, 64
Pictures at an Exhibition, VI:105
Pierrot Lunaire, VI:170
Pike, Lipman, X:125 ff
"Pilpul," IX: 63
Ping-pong, X:24
Pinsker, Yehuda Leib, II:230, 237; IX:125 ff
Pissarro, Camille, III:105 ff
Pithom, I:25
Pittsburgh Pirates, X:40, 56, 60, 112
Piyyut, I:136
Plain of Jezreel, VII:56
Planck Prize, Max, IV:88
Planets, V:48
Playwriting, VI:124
Plehve, von, II:238
Pliny, I:107
Plutonium, IV:154; V:126, 128
Poale Zion (Labor Zionist Party), II:239; VIII:38, 184
Podolia, II:226, 227
Poland, Jews in, I:151 ff, 158, 163 ff; II:190, 192, 194, 196, 198, 199, 200, 209, 211, 226, 227, 235, 236, 256, 265, 268, 279, 288, 292
Polio, V:104, 106, 112
Poliomyelitis virus, V:104, 108
Polish Underground, VII:92
Polybius, I:85
Pompey, I:99-102; VII:30
Pontius Pilate, I:111
Pope Innocent X, V:68
Pope Sextus IV, VIII:14
Popular Front, The French, VIII:46
Porgy and Bess, VI:58
Portrait for Orchestra—Mark Twain, VI:102
Portugal, VIII:84, 174; Jews in, I:150, 151, 153, 163; II:187, 190, 191
Portuguese Jews, Amsterdam, II:212
Positrons, IV:150
Poulenc, Francois, VI:120
Powell, Dick, VI:42
Poznan, I:203, 213
Prague, II:189, 193, 198, 203, 213, 215
Preakness, The, X:122
Prinstein, Myer, X:129 ff
Princeton Tigers, X:82
Princeton University, X:82
Princeton University, Institute for Advanced Study, IV:52, 132
Prittie, Terence, VII:34
Problem of Disarmament, The, IV:63
Prokofieff, Serge, VI:105
Promenade Concerts, VI:102
Prophet, The, VI:118
Provence, II:180, 181, 184
Provisional Committee for General Zionist Affairs, VIII:48
Prussia, II:195, 196, 207, 208
Psalms, Book of, VII:46
Psammetichus, I:59
Psychoanalysis, V:36 ff
Ptolemies, I:82, 88, 99, 108
Pulitzer Prize, VI:68, 124, 127
Pumbeditha, I:143, 159
Puritans, II:243, 244

Q

Qalqilya, II:338
Quantum Mechanics Theory, IV:54, 55, 56, 156
Quarennial Diet, VII:158
Qumran, I:98

R

Rab (Abba Arikha), I:142
Rabad (Abraham Ibn Daud), II:182
Rabi, Isidor, IV:135 ff
Rabin, Yitzhak, VII:121 ff
Rabinowitz, Solomon, see Aleichem, Shalom
"Race of Nations", X:114
Rachel, Tribes, I:29
"Racing Club", X:114
Radical Socialist Party, France, VIII:124
Radio, VI:62
Radio City Music Hall, VI:142, 166
Radio Corporation of America, V:114-16
Radioactivity, V:128
Rafiah, II:304
Ramat Rachel, I:79; II:274, 295
Rambam (Maimonides, Moses), IX:113 ff, 118
Ramle, II:303
Ramses, city, I:25
Ramses II, I:25, 28, 29
Ramses III, I:30, 31
Rashba (Rabbi Shelmo Ben Adreth), I:162
Rashi, I:159, 163; II:185, 186; IX:129 ff
Rathenau, Emil, IV:70
Rathenau, Walter, VIII:151 ff
Ravel, Maurice, VI:105
Raziel, David, VII:127 ff, 142
Reading, Lord, II:280
Realism, III:62, 74
Recife, II:242, 243
Reconstructionism, II:251
Red Guard, VII:134
Red Petticoat, The, VI:96
Red Sea, I:37, 39; II:303
Reflections on the Revolution of Our Time, VIII:108
Reform Judaism, II:217, 245, 247, 249; IX:92, 94
Reformation, Protestant, II:193, 194
Refugees, II:330
Regensburg, II:187
Rehoboam, I:37, 38
Rehovot, II:325
Reichstein, Tadeusz, IV:141 ff
Reines, Rabbi Isaac Jacob, IX:133 ff
Reinhardt, Max, VI:145 ff, 186
Reisebriefe aus Eretz Israel (Travel Notes on Palestine), VIII:76
Relativity, Theory of, IV:48, 50, 52, 122, 124
Rembrandt, III:43, 62
Renoir, III:112
Rephaim, I:14
Republican Party, VIII:104, 106
Reshevsky, Samuel, X:46, 133 ff
Resin, IV:163
Resistance Fighters, VII:20, 92, 94
Respiration, IV:166
Retina transplant, V:142
Reuben, Tribe, I:29
Revel, Rabbi Bernard, II:248, 252
Revisionist Movement, II:274; VIII:96
Revolts, Jewish, VII:20 ff, 30 ff, 98 ff
Rezin, I:50
Rhapsody in Blue, VI:56, 88
Rheinische Zeitung, IX:89
Rheumatic Diseases, IV:142
Rh Factor, IV:92
Rhineland, I:157, 158, 162, 164
Rhodes, I:104, II:304
Riad, Mahmoud, II:332
Ribicoff, Abraham A., VIII:159 ff
Ribonucleic acid, IV:78
Rice, Grantland, X:52
Rickover, Hyman, V:97 ff
Rieser, Gabriel, II:214
Rise of European Liberalism, The, VIII:110
Rivera, Diego, III:86
RNA, IV:78
Road of Orange, A, III:55
Robert the Devil, VI:116
Roberta, VI:96
Robinson, Edward G., VI:149 ff
Rockefeller Foundation, IV:110
Rockefeller Institute for Medical Research, IV:92
Rockne, Knute, X:52, 54
Rodgers, Richard, VI:155 ff
Rodin, III:40, 86
Rodzinski, Artur, VI:34, 98
Roman rule of Palestine, VII:30
Romans, Roman Empire, I:76, 83, 88 (map), 98, 99, 102, 111, 112, 123, 126, 128, 132, 134, 141, 157; II:327
Romanticism, III:52; IV:74
Rome, I:108, 141, 145, 150
Rothenberg, I:162, 163
Rothschild, House of, II:213, 217, 238
Romberg, Sigmund, VI:66
Rome and Jerusalem, IX:89
Rommel, Field Marshal Erwin, VII:12, 136

Roof Jewish Philanthropies, VIII:106
Roosevelt, Franklin D., III:158; IV:24, 52, 170; V:132; VII:104; VIII:20, 24, 116, 133, 134; IX:142, 170
Roosevelt, Franklin D. Jr., VIII:104
Roosevelt, Theodore, VIII:48, 82
Rose Marie, VI:66
Rose Mauri, X:137 ff
Rosenberg, Max, VI:56
Rosenzweig, Franz, IX:54
Rosh Hashanah, X:58
Ross, Barney, X:106, 139 ff
Rothschild Family, III:100
Roualt, III:104
Rovina, Hannah, VI:159 ff
Royal Association of Astronomy, V:48
Royal Philharmonic Orchestra, VI:179
Royal Society of London, VI:106
Rubashov, Shneour Zalman, see Shneour Zalman Shazar, VIII:183 ff
Rubin, Reuven, III:113, 122
Rubinstein, Artur, VI:163 ff
Rubinstein, Louis, X:143 ff
Rumania, Jews in, II:208, 211, 219, 238, 256, 268
Runner of Afek, The, X:147 ff
Runyon, Damon, X:17
Russel, Hamilton Trophy, X:136
Russell, Bertrand, V:150
Russell, Bill, X:20, 21
Russia, Jews in, I:157; II:196, 199, 209, 212, 216, 219, 233, 239, 256, 265, 268, 276, 282, 288, 306, 310
Russian Government Prize, IV:58
Russian Revolution of 1905, VI:152; VIII:38
Russian Revolution of 1917, II:210, 256, 265; IV:128
Russian Symphony Orchestra, VI:53
Russo-Japanese War, VII:152
Ruth the Moabite, VII:42
Rutherford, Ernest, IV:30, 87
Ruzicka, Leopold, IV:142

S

Sabin, Albert Bruce, V:103 ff, 108
Sachs, Nelly, IV:145 ff
Sacred Service, VI:40, 120
Sadeh, Yitzhak, VII:12, 133 ff
St. John's University, X:34
St. Louis Brown Stockings, X:127
St. Louis Cardinals (Football), X:56
St. Petersburg Academy, III:42
St. Petersburg Conservatory, VI:52, 70
St. Stephen's Gate, II:339
Sale of Personal Property, VIII:36
Salk, Jonas Edward, V:104, 107 ff
Salk's vaccine, V:104, 108
Salon, The, III:111
Salversan, IV:44
Samson, VII:137 ff
Samuel, VII:44
Samuel, Herbert, VIII:165 ff
San Francisco Conservatory of Music, VI:40, 178
San Francisco Symphony, VI:178
Sand, George, VI:26
Sangari, VIII:176
Sanhedrin (Supreme Council of the Jews), VIII:137
Santa Anita, X:32
Saratoga Handicap, X:122
Sarnoff, David, V:113 ff
Satel, Albert, IV:158
Satie, Erik, VI:120
Saudades de Brazil, VI:120
Saudi Arabia, II:334
Saul, VII:42, 44
Savitt, Dick, X:151 ff
Scarlet Fever, V:180
Schapira, Hermann Tzevi, VIII:169
Schatz (Zalman Dov) Boris, III:117 ff
Schayes, Adolph, X:155 ff
Schick, Bela, V:117 ff
Schneider, Guenther, VI:12
Schoenberg, Arnold, VI:167 ff
Schoepp, Franz, VI:60
The School for Women, VI:26
Schroeder, Ted, X:152
Schwartz, Maurice, VI:173 ff
Schwarz, David, V:121 ff
Scholem, Gershom, IV:134
Screen Actors Guild, VI:18
Scribe, Eugene, VI:116
Seaborg, Dr. Glenn T., IV:154
Second sound, IV:88
Second String Quartet, VI:168, 170
Second Temple, IX:63
The Secret Life of Walter Mitty, VI:92
Sedran, Barney, X:66, 159 ff
Segre, Emilio Gino, IV:149 ff
Selim, VIII:137
Senate, U.S., VIII:104
Set theory, V:24
Seventy-Sixers, The, X:158
Severus, Julius, VII:32

Severus, kings, I:130
Seville, X:48, 50
Sezession Der Berlin, III:78
Shabbetai, II:201, 226, 227, 229
Shahn, Ben, III:123 ff
Shakespeare, IV:128
Shalmaneser III, I:39, 40
Shalmaneser IV, I:50
Shalom Aleichem, *see* Aleichem, Shalom
Shamgar, I:30
Shaprut, Hasdai Ibn, VIII:173
Shapur I, I:142
Sharett, Moshe, II:279; VIII:177 ff, 186
Sharm-el-Sheikh, II:332
Sharon, valley, I:30, 77
Shaveh Kiniathaim, I:14
Shaw, Wilbur, X:138
Shazar, Schneour Zalman, II:311; VIII:183 ff
Shealtiel, I:76
Shearith Israel Synagogue, II:251
Sheba ben Bichri, I:35, 37
Sheba, Queen of, I:37
Shechem, I:28, 30, 32, 37, 79; VII:70
Shelomo, VI:38
Shelomo ben Adreth (*see* Rashba)
Shephelah, I:29, 49
Shertok, Moshe, *see* Moshe Sharett
Sheshbazzar, I:75
Shield of David (Mogen David), VII:18
Shiloh, I:32, 34, 35
Shimon bar Yizhak, Rabbi, II:184
Shimon bar Yokhai, Rabbi, II:184
Shimon ben Gamliel, Rabbi, I:127-130
Shinwell, Emanuel, VIII:189
Shishak, I:38
Shmuel ben Hophni, II:183
Shmuel Halevi, Rabbi, I:156, 164
Shmuel, Hanagid, II:179
Shneour Zalman of Lyady, II:228; IX:137 ff
Shoshanim, II:178
Shrine of the Book, IX:172
Show Boat, VI:66, 96, 98
Shukairy, Ahmed, II:332, 334
Shulchan Aruch (The Prepared Table), II:200; IX:58 ff, 140
Shylock, I:148
Sicily, I:159
Sick War, The, IV:62
Sidom, I:35, 84
Sihon, Sihonites, I:27, 28, 29
Siloam tunnel, I:54, 55
Silver, Abba Hillel, IX:141 ff
Silver Skates, X:74
Simeon, *see also* Shimon
Simeon, tribe, I:15, 28, 29
Simon Bolivar, VI:122
Simon Maccabeus, I:98, 99
Simson, Sampson, II:224
Sinai campaign, II:309, 310; VII:54, 122; VIII:30
Sinai, I:16, 25, 26; II:334, 337, 338, 339, 340; VIII:30; IX:50
Sisera, I:30; VII:56
Les Six, VI:120
Six Day War, II:321 ff; blockade of Gulf of Aqaba, 322; cease-fire, 340, 343; international reaction: American, 332, 334, 337; British, 332, 334, 337; Canadian, 332; French, 346; Russian, 331, 332, 338, 346; reunification of Jerusalem, 338, 344; V:80; VII:54, 122 ff; VIII:66, 68
Six Pieces for Piano, VI:170
Slotin, Louis, V:129 ff
Smith, Harry, X:164
Smoke Gets in Your Eyes, VI:96
Smyslow, Vassily, X:136
Sobey, James, III:124
Sobibor, II:292
Soccer, X:24, 66
Social Democratic Party, VIII:114
Socialism, VIII:108 ff
Sofer, Hatam, IX:145 ff
So Help Me, VI:84
Solomon, I:36, 37, 40, 49, 52; VII:46
Song of Songs, V:68
Song to Remember, A, VI:132
The Sound of Music, VI:67
Sound waves, V:65
South Africa, Jews in, II:281
South Pacific, VI:67
Soutine, Chaim, III:127 ff
Soviet literature, IV:128
Soviet Union, *see* Russia
Soviet Writers' Association, IV:128
Space Committee of the National Defense Research Council, IV:38
Spain, Jews in, I:141, 147-150, 151, 152, 153, 154, 157, 162, 163, 166, 168; II:177-182, 184, 185, 187, 188, 190, 191; VIII:12, 84, 136 ff, 174, 176
Sparta, X:148
Spiers, I:164
Spinoza, Baruch, II:202; IX:149 ff
Stalin, Josef, II:256
Stalin Prize, VI:138

State in Theory and Practice, The, VIII:110
Staudinger, Herman, IV:142
Steel Highway, VI:42
Steinberg, Morris, X:134
Steinhardt, Jacob, III:133 ff
Steinitz, William, X:94
Steinman, David B., V:133 ff
Steinmetz, Charles, V:139 ff
Abraham Stern, VII:130, 141 ff
Stern Gang, VII:142
Stern, Isaac, VI:177 ff
Stern, Otto, IV:155 ff
Stein, Yossi, III:139 ff
Stettin, II:290
Stevenson, Adlai, VIII:72
Stilling, Benedict, V:145 ff
Stradonitz, Friedrich August Kepule von, IV:162
Straits of Tiran, II:332
Strassburg, II:212
Stravinsky, Igor, VI:105
Street Scene, VI:188
Streisand, Barbra, VI:181 ff
Streptomycin, IV:158, 159, 160
String Quartet in D Minor, VI:168
Struck, Hermann, III:145 ff
Stuyvesant, Peter, II:244
Submarine, atomic, V:98, 99
Sudan, II:334, 337
Suez Canal, II:310, 330, 339, 346; VIII:58
Sufferings of Israel, IV:146
Suffolk Downs, IX:70
Sullivan, Ed, VI:20
Sulzberger, Mayer, II:249
Summertime, VI:58
Sunday Afternoon Symphony Concert, VI:36
Sunny, VI:96
Supreme Court, VIII:72
Sura, I:142, 143, 159
Surgery, V:142
Survivor from Warsaw, A, VI:170
Switzerland, Jews in, II:218
Susa (Shushan), I:78
Swedish Literature, IV:146
Swimming, X:62
Symphonic Jazz, VI:58
Synagogues' Council of England, VIII:128
Synchro-cyclotron, IV:150
Syphilis, IV:44
Syracuse University, X:130
Syria, I:12, 15, 27, 35, 36, 38-50, 54, 58, 74, 77, 84, 87, 102, 107, 108, 111, 125, 126, 141; II:299, 300, 302, 309, 330, 311, 332, 337, 340, 343; VII:36 ff, 48, 54, 98, 112
Szenes, Hanna, VII:147 ff
Szilard, Leo, IV:170
Szold, Henrietta, II:248, 280; IX:153 ff
Szyk, Arthur, III:151 ff

T

Table-Tennis, X:24
Tacitus, I:125
Tales of Hoffman, The, VI:136
Tales of Jochanan The Melamed, The, IX:122
Tales of the Hasidim, IX:56
Talmud, I:124, 125, 141, 142, 143, 159, 166; II:178-181,, 183, 185, 186, 219
Tam, Rabbenu Yaakov, II:163, 164
Tannaim, I:123, 128
Tartars, V:17
Tchernichovsky, Saul, II:219; IX:159 ff
Technion, II:325; IV:60
Tel Aviv, II:270, 279, 297, 298, 300, 302, 303, 306, 324, 325, 326
Tel Aviv Museum, III:50, 116
Telegraph, V:64
Telephone, V:20, 64
Television, V:115, 116
Tel-Hai, VII:154, 156
Teller, Edward, V:96, 149 ff
Tel-Qasile, I:40
Tel Yosef, II:266
Temple, First, I:36, 37, 49, 54, 57, 58, 59, 62
Temple, Second, I:75-79, 85, 88, 97, 102, 104, 105-107, 109, 111, 122-128, 131, 133, 141
Temple of Solomon, V:80
Temple Tiferet Israel, IX:144
Tennis, X:98, 152
Terahites, I:15
Territorialists, II:236, 237
Terrorism, II:330, 331
Tevye the Milkman, IX:16
Texas League, X:86
Texeira, II:197
Theatre Guild Award, VI:124
Theima, I:74
Thekel, I:30
Theodotus, I:102

Theory of Organic Chemistry, The, IV:38
Theory of Relativity, V:24
Thermos bottle, V:76
The Third Little Show, VI:12
This Is the Army, VI:22
Thirty Years War, II:192
Thorium explosions, V:86
Threepenny Opera, The, VI:186
Thut-Mose IV (Thotmes), I:26
Thyroid gland, IV:102
Tiberias, I:106, 134; II:297, 300, 302, 327; VIII:136, 137, 138; IX:116
Ticho, Hannah, III:122
Tiglath-Pileser III, I:49, 58
Time, Bergson's Theory of, IV:22
Tinker, Joe, X:86, 88
Titanic, V:114
Titus, I:108, 110
Tobacco, V:70
Tobiads, I:75, 83
Todd, Mike, VI:42
Todros, Rav, I:166
Toledo, I:156, 162, 164
Tonight We Sing, VI:180
Torquemada, Tomas de, I:150
Tosafot, II:186
Toscanini, Arturo, VI:76, 142
Toten Leider, IV:74
Touro, Judah, VIII:130
Town Hall, VI:178
Trachonitis, I:105
Track, X:12, 114, 130
Tragedy, Modern, VI:127
Trajan, I:122, 123, 141; VII:30
Transduction, IV:96
Transfinite numbers, V:26
Transjordan, I:12, 14, 27-30, 35, 36, 39-49, 64, 77, 84, 86, 99, 102, 105, 106; VIII:96
Transjordan frontier force, II:298
Travers, X:122
Treasury Department, VIII:134
Treaty of Rapallo, VIII:154
Treblinka, II:292
Tree Grows in Brooklyn, A, VI:42
Triangle, Arab, II:302
Triborough Bridge, V:130
Troyes, II:185
Troy Haymakers, The, X:127
Truman, Harry S., II:306
Trumpeldor, Joseph, II:273; VII:134, 155 ff; VIII:96
Tsaddikim (Righteous men), IX:56, 140
Tsalmona, VII:70
Tudela, II:187
Tunisia, II:337
Turkey, Turks, I:154; II:226; VIII:137
Turkish Rule of Palestine, VII:26, 114, 152
Typhus, IV:158
Tyre, I:35, 36, 37, 39, 40

U

Ukraine, Jews in, I:157; II:256
Ulpan, II:308, 325
Union for Peace, IV:62
Union of American Hebrew Congregations, II:247
Union of Orthodox Jewish Congregations, II:245
United Jewish Appeal, IV:52; VI:132; VIII:132; IX:142; X:170
United Nations, II:296, 298, 303, 304, 306, 308, 310, 334; IV:140, 172; VIII:62, 64, 72, 74, 76, 180, 187; Atomic Energy Commission, VIII:24; Emergency Force, II:332; Political Committee, V:32; Relief and Rehabilitation Administration (UNRRA), VIII:116, 118; Security Council, II:331, 338, 339, 346; Truce Supervision Organization, II:331
United States Davis Cup Team, X:152
United States, government, VIII:102 ff, 132 ff, 160 ff
United States of America, Jews in, II:208, 211, 213, 218, 239, 242, 243-254, 256, 268, 270, 276, 278, 280-282, 306, 309, 324, 325
United Synagogue Council, VII:120
United Synagogue of America, II:251, 252
Up in Arms, VI:92
Ur, I:14, 25
Uranium, IV:32, 136, 154; V:86
Uranus, V:48
Uriah, VII:46
Uri Brenner, VII:136
Ur-Nammu, I:25
Ursicinus, I:133
Ussischkin, Menahem, II:230, 278
U Thant, II:332, 334; VIII:184
Uzziah, I:49, 50

V

Vaad Leumi, II:272-275
Venosa, 167
Versailles, treaty of, 236, 268, 269, 286
Vespasianus, I:110, 111, 126
Victoria, Queen, VIII:58, 59, 128
Vienna, I:191, 195, 203, 210, 213, 234, 290
Vilna, Gaon of, 229

W

Waddell, Rube, X:40
Wagner, Honus, X:40
Wagner, Robert F., VIII:104, 118
Wagon Train, VI:42
Wailing Wall, V:80; IX:86
Waksman, Selman Abraham, IV:157 ff
Wallach, Otto, IV:161 ff
Walter, Bruno, VI:36, 114
Wannsee, conference, II:292
Warburg, Felix, II:278; IV:166
Warburg, Otto Heinrich, IV:80, 165 ff
Warburg's Yellow Enzyme, IV:166
War of Independence, Israel's, VII:14, 34, 52, 104, 122 ff; VIII:30; IX:176
War Industries Board, U.S.A., VIII:22, 24
Warsaw, II:287, 289, 293
Warsaw Ghetto, III:36; VII:20 ff, 34 ff
Washington, George University, X:22
Wave length measurement, V:65
Wave theory of light, IV:105
Weightlifting, X:28
Weill, Kurt, VI:185 ff
Weimar Republic, VIII:153
Weiner, Dr. Alexander Solomon, IV:92
Weisberg, Nahum, VI:174
Weiss, Erich, *see* Houdini, VI:78
Weizmann, Chaim, II:238, 272, 276, 278, 279, 280, 307; IV:52; VII:88, 90; VIII:18, 41, 62, 78, 96, 168, 193 ff; IX:54, 142, 144
Weizmann Institute of Science, II:325; V:33; VIII:63, 200
Wellington, VII:110
Wene, Sylvia, X:163 ff
Western League, X:86
Western Union, V:21
Western Wall, *see* Wailing Wall
West Point, VII:104, 108
West Side Story, VI:36
Whistling in the Dark, VI:12
White Christmas, VI:22
White Paper on Palestine, of 1939, II:275, 278
Whitney, John Hay, VIII:104
Who?, VI:68
Why Do I Love You, VI:68, 96
Wiener, Norbert W., V:153 ff
Wigner, Eugene Paul, IV:169 ff
Willstatter, Richard, IV:173 ff; V:28
Wilson, Don, VI:18
Wilson's cloud chamber, IV:66, 68
Wilson, Woodrow, VIII:20, 51, 81; IX:170
Wimbledon, X:98, 100, 152
Wingate, Col. Orde, II:275; VII:48
Wireless telegraph, V:14, 54, 64
Wisconsin, University of, X:83, 84
Wise, Rabbi Isaac Mayer, II:247, 252; IX:163 ff
Wise, Dr. Stephen, II:271; IX:167 ff
Wittenberg, Henry, X:167 ff
Wohlgemuth, I:149
Woman Called Hannah, A, IX:122
Wonder Man, The, VI:92
Woodcarving, III:164
World Atomic Physicists, IV:171
World Bank, II:325
World Jewish Congress, II:271; VIII:78, 132; IX:170
World Series, X:40, 41
World War I, III:34, 54; IV:63, 70, 128, 174; VII:72, 88, 114; VIII:48, 66, 146, 152
World War II, III:36, 46; IV:32, 58, 146; V:94; VII:12, 72, 74, 86, 90, 104, 118, 130, 136, 148; VIII:62, 66, 122
World Zionist organization, II:236-239, 252, 274-276, 278, 279; VII:90; VIII:76, 78, 94, 200
Worms, I:159, 164; II:185
Worms Synagogue, VI:130
Wrestling, X:168
Wurttemberg, prince of, II:192

Y

Yadin, Yigal, II:300; IX:171 ff
Yad Mordechai, II:302
Yale University, X:54

Yarmuk, I:29
Yathrib, I:74
Yavneh, I:106, 127
Yeb, I:77
Yehiam, II:298
Yehoash, IX:124
Yehosef, I:161
Yehuda I, Rabbi, I:130, 132, 142
Yehuda II, Rabbi, I:130, 132
Yehuda Halevi, Rabbi, I:146; II:182, 186, 187
Yehuda Hizkiah, I:107
Yehuda, Liwa ben Bezalel (Maharal), II:193
Yellow Enzyme, Warburg's, IV:166
Yemen, II:184, 281, 308, 323, 324, 337
Yeshiva University, II:248, 252, 253
Yevseksia, II:265
Yiddish, II:214, 219, 220, 223, 235, 236, 251
Yiddish Art Theater, VI:130, 174, 176
Yishuv, II:267, 270-276, 279, 280, 282, 296, 298
Yoash, VII:68
Yoelson, Asa, VI:86
Yohanan ben Levi, I:107
Yohanan ben Zakkai, Rabbi, I:127
Yohiyezer, I:79
Yom Kippur, IX:96; X:59, 60, 90
Yoreh Deah, IV:59
Yoselevitz, Berek, VII:157 ff
Ysaye, Eugene, VI:38, 166

Z

Zachariah, I:76
Zamenhof, Ludwig, IX:177 ff
Zangwill, Israel, II:239, 280; VIII:91
Zatopek, Emil, X:114
Zealots, I:107, 109, 111, 133; VII:30
Zebulun, tribe, I:29; VII:56
Zechariah's tomb, I:88
Zedekiah, I:59, 63
Zeppelin, V:122
Zerubabel, I:75, 76
Zevach, VII:70
Zichron Moshe, VIII:130
Ziggurat of Ur, I:25
Zionides ("Songs of Zion"), IX:84, 86
Zionism, II:217, 220, 231, 236-239, 247, 251-253, 256, 265, 268, 269, 273, 280, 281; IV:52; VII:66, 152; VIII:16, 88 ff, 96 ff, 144 ff; IX:13, 14, 54
Zionist Congresses, II:232-234, 238, 272, 273, 278, 281, 322; First, VIII:172
Zionist General Council VIII:16
Zionist Organization of America, VIII:48, 106; IX:170
Zion Mule Corps, VII:154; VIII:96
Zola, Emile, VI:132; VII:64
Zorach, William, III:163 ff
Zoroastrians, I:142
Zurich, II:278
Zuzim, I:14
Zvi, Ben, III:122

PICTURE CREDITS

American Friends of Hebrew University, V:80, 81
American Jewish Archives, III:35, 47, 147; IV:47, 51; V:35; VI:27, 71, 87, 113; VII:29, 113; VIII:19, 22, 33, 45, 47, 50, 71; IX:51, 168; X:13
Shlomo Arad, Tel Aviv, III:53
AP Newsfeatures Photo, VIII:35, 121
Leo Baeck Institute, IX:21, 23
Bettman Archive, V:27, 51, 123, 124, 131, 143; VII:41, 97; VIII:13, 55
Boy Scouts of America, VIII:106
Herbert Braun, Israel, IX:155
B.B.C. Publications, London, III:157; IV:114; V:91; VI:82, 83, 95, 151, 153; VII:55, 59, 61, 63, 64, 65, 71, 73; VIII:107, 109, 123, 125, 157, 189; IX:150, 179
British Museum, VIII:57, 60, 127; X:119
Brown Brothers, IV:21, 50, 73; V:21
City College of the City University of New York, VIII:21
Harry A. Cole, IX:141
Columbia Pictures, VI:14, 124, 183
Columbia Records, VI:99, 101
Culver Pictures, Inc., III:152, 153, 155, 161, 163; IV:113, 115; V:73, 107, 109, 137, 138, 139; VI:29, 63, 97; VII:109, 111; VIII:117; X:101, 103
Dover Publications, V:23
Foto Custodia Terra Santa, VII:58
Friedman-Abeles, IX:17, 19
Gabinetto Fotografico, Florence, IX:112
Henry Gross, VIII:25
Alexander Guttmann, IX:25
A. Haozar, Jerusalem, III:139
D. Harris—W. Braun, Jerusalem, VII:31
W. Herz, Jerusalem, III:137
Hurok Attractions, VI:141, 163, 165, 177, 179
IBM, V:151
International Photo, VI:37
Israel Information Service, V:37; VIII:187
Israel Office of Information, VII:103, 123
George Jervas, VIII:101
Jewish Agency, Jerusalem, III:142; VII:85, 155; IX:167
Jewish National Fund, VIII:169
Jewish Theological Seminary, IX:65, 67, 69
Keren Hayesod United Israel Appeal, VIII:17, 75, 155; IX:97, 161
Keystone Press Agency, London, IV:81, 83, 138, 151, 156, 159; VI:45, 51, 65, 73, 84, 103, 106, 107, 150, 152, 157; VIII:131, 133, 156
March of Dimes, V:103, 105, 111
Matson Photo Service, VII:45
MGM, VI:11
Metropolitan Museum of Art, IX:110
K. Meyerowitz, Jerusalem, IV:23

Th. Modin, IV:93
Movie Star News., IV:127; VI:13, 15, 50, 81, 89, 92, 125
Museum of Modern Art, III:165
New York Philharmonic, VI:33, 34, 35
Nobel Foundation, IV:35, 53, 55, 61, 79, 85, 103, 131, 135, 141, 143, 147 149, 155, 169, 173
Oriental Institute, University of Chicago, VII:57, 139; VIII:139, 140
Photohouse Prior, Tel Aviv, VI:31, 121, 143, 187; VII:21, 37
RCA News, V:113, 116
Ring Magazine, X:15, 17, 35, 107, 117, 141
RKO Radio Pictures, VI:93
David Rubinger, Jerusalem, III:140
S. J. Schweiz, Jerusalem, V:82
Harry Simonhoff, V:19
Ricky Smith, VII:119
Spalding Basketball Advisory Staff, X:157
Twentieth Century Fox, VII:117
Union of American Hebrew Congregations, IX:163
United Artists, VI:41
UNICEF, VI:94
UPI, IV:29, 59, 67, 77, 117, 119, 121, 157; V:85, 97, 121, 145, 149; VI:55, 69, 85, 111, 129, 131, 149; VIII:79, 115, X:9, 27, 29, 31, 43, 45, 47, 49, 51, 53, 55, 57, 59 61, 65, 67, 69, 71, 73, 75, 81, 83, 85, 87, 89, 91, 93, 97, 99, 109, 111, 133, 135, 151, 153, 167, 169
Photo Marc Vaux, Paris, III:101
H. Roger Viollet, IV:15, 69, 161; VI:47, 135; VIII:141, 165, 167
S. H. Waksman, Rutgers University Press, V:46
Conrad Waldinger, VIII:23
Warner Bros., VI:19
K. Weiss, Jerusalem, V:83
Westinghouse Photo, V:33
Whitestone Photo., VIII:67
Wide World Photos., III:33; IV:19, 25, 26, 27, 31, 33, 37, 41, 42, 71, 91, 95, 97, 100, 101, 107, 109, 110, 126, 129, 133, 137, 139, 152, 153, 167, 171, 172, 175; V:40, 41, 99, 100, 101, 110, 117, 119, 129, 131, 133, 134, 135, 140, 146, 147; VI:17, 43, 54, 77, 79, 119, 122, 125, 137, 139, 140, 147, 167, 169, 171, 173; VII:39, 53, 129; VIII:73, 74, 153, 161, 163; X:21, 23, 25, 33, 34, 39, 41, 63, 105, 121, 123, 127, 163, 165
Yivo, III:22, 23, 51, 57, 58, 117, 119, 151, 154; VI:123, 175; VIII:123, 129
Zionist Archives, III:17, 56, 134, 145; VII:22, 49, 50, 57, 87, 89, 94, 95, 100, 106, 144, 145, 149; VIII:27, 28, 29, 32, 40, 41, 42, 64, 69, 77, 89, 90, 91, 95, 97, 98, 99, 117, 145, 179, 181, 186, 195, 197, 198; IX:20, 50, 81, 116, 121, 143, 169, 175